P9-CBC-212

Rosa Parks and the Montgomery Bus Boycott

Lucent Library of Black History

Lydia Bjornlund

LUCENT BOOKS

An imprint of Thomson Gale, a part of The Thomson Corporation

THOMSON

GALE

Detroit • New York • San Francisco • New Haven, Conn. • Waterville, Maine • London

For more information, contact
Lucent Books
27500 Drake Rd.
Farmington Hills, MI 48331-3535
Or you can visit our Internet site at http://www.gale.com

LIBRARY OF CONGRESS CATALOGING-IN-PUBLICATION DATA

Bjornlund, Lydia D.
  Rosa Parks and the Montgomery Bus Boycott / by Lydia Bjornlund.
    p. cm. — (Lucent library of Black history)
Includes bibliographical references and index.
  ISBN-13: 978-1-4205-0010-3 (hardcover)
1. Parks, Rosa, 1913-2005—Juvenile literature. 2. Montgomery Bus Boycott, Montgomery, Ala., 1955–1956—Juvenile literature. 3. African Americans—Civil rights—Alabama—Montgomery—History—20th century—Juvenile literature. 4. Segregation in transportation—Alabama—Montgomery—History—20th century— Juvenile literature. 5. Civil rights movements—Alabama—Montgomery—History—20th century—Juvenile literature. 6. Montgomery (Ala.)—Race relations—History—20th century—Juvenile literature. 7. African American civil rights workers—Alabama— Montgomery—Biography —Juvenile literature. 8. African American women— Alabama—Montgomery—Biography—Juvenile literature. 9. Montgomery (Ala.)— Biography—Juvenile literature. I. Title.
  F334.M753P38245 2007
  323.092—dc22

[B]

2007024048

ISBN-10: 1-4205-0010-4

Printed in the United States of America

Contents

Foreword   4

Introduction
Rosa Parks Refuses to Move   6

Chapter One
Life in the Jim Crow South   10

Chapter Two
Seeds of Resistance   27

Chapter Three
The Boycott Begins   42

Chapter Four
The Boycott Continues   56

Chapter Five
Victory   71

Notes   88
Chronology   94
For More Information   96
Index   99
Picture Credits   103
About the Author   104

Foreword

It has been more than 500 years since Africans were first brought to the New World in shackles, and over 140 years since slavery was formally abolished in the United States. Over 50 years have passed since the fallacy of "separate but equal" was obliterated in the American courts, and some forty years since the watershed Civil Rights Act of 1965 guaranteed the rights and liberties of all Americans, especially those of color. Over time, these changes have become celebrated landmarks in American history. In the twenty-first century, African American men and women are politicians, judges, diplomats, professors, deans, doctors, artists, athletes, business owners, and home owners. For many, the scars of the past have melted away in the opportunities that have been found in contemporary society. Observers such as Peter N. Kirsanow, who sits on the U.S. Commission of Civil Rights, point to these accomplishments and conclude, "The growing black middle class may be viewed as proof that most of the civil rights battles have been won."

In spite of these legal victories, however, prejudice and inequality have persisted in American society. In 2003, African Americans comprised just 12 percent of the nation's population, yet accounted for 44 percent of its prison inmates and 24 percent of its poor. Racially motivated hate crimes continue to appear on the pages of major newspapers in many American cities. Furthermore, many African Americans still experience either overt or muted racism in their daily lives. A 1996 study undertaken by Professor Nancy Krieger of the Harvard School of Public Health, for example, found that 80 percent of the African American participants reported having experienced racial discrimination in one or more settings, including at work or school, applying for housing and medical care, from the police or in the courts, and on the street or in a public setting.

It is for these reasons that many believe the struggle for racial equality and justice is far from over. These episodes of discrimination threaten to shatter the illusion that America has completely overcome its racist past, causing many black Americans to become increasingly frustrated and confused. Scholar and writer Ellis Cose has described this splintered state in the following way: "I have done everything I was supposed to do. I have stayed out of trouble with the law, gone to the right schools, and worked myself nearly to death. What more do they want? Why in God's name won't they accept me as a full human being?" For Cose and others, the struggle for equality and justice has yet to be fully achieved.

In many subtle yet important ways the traumatic experiences of slavery and segregation continue to inform the way race is discussed and experienced in the twenty-first century. Indeed, it is possible that America will always grapple with the fallout from its distressing past. Ulric Haynes, dean of the Hofstra University School of Business has said, "Perhaps race will always matter, given the historical circumstances under which we came to this country." But studying this past and understanding how it contributes to present-day dialogues about race and history in America is a critical component of contemporary education. To this end, the Lucent Library of Black History offers a thorough look at the experiences that have shaped the black community and the American people as a whole. Annotated bibliographies provide readers with ideas for further research, while fully documented primary and secondary source quotations enhance the text. Each book in the series explores a different episode of black history; together they provide students with a wealth of information as well as launching points for further study and discussion.

Rosa Parks Refuses to Move

On December 1, 1955, after a long day of work as a seamstress in Montgomery, Alabama, Rosa Parks prepared to take the bus home as always. When the bus arrived at her stop, she stepped up the stairs, plunked a dime into the fare box, got back off the bus, and reentered by the rear door. The bus was crowded, but Parks found a seat on the aisle a few rows from the back.

Two stops later, all of the seats in the whites-only section at the front of the bus were taken, leaving a white man standing in the aisle. The bus driver asked the four people in Parks's row to stand so the white man could sit. At first, no one moved. "You all make it light on yourselves and let me have those seats," the driver demanded. The man sitting between Parks and the window stood up and squeezed past her to stand in the aisle. The two women across the aisle also stood. But Rosa Parks kept her seat.

The driver asked her if she was going to stand up. "No, I'm not," Parks responded.

"Well if you don't stand up, I'm going to call the police and have you arrested."

"You may do that," responded Parks.[1]

The driver got off the bus to call the police, and Rosa Parks waited calmly. She recalled later:

> As I sat there, I tried not to think about what might happen. I knew that anything was possible. I could be manhandled or beaten. I could be arrested. People have asked me if it occurred to me then that I could be the test case the NAACP [National Association for the Advancement of Colored People] had been looking for. I did not think about that at all. In fact if I had let myself think too deeply about what might happen to me, I might have gotten off the bus.[2]

Two police officers got on the bus and asked her why she did not stand up when the driver told her to. "Why do you all push us around?" she replied.

"I don't know, but the law is the law, and you're under arrest,"[3] said the policeman, who then escorted her off the bus.

Segregation signs like this one, found on a North Carolina bus, appeared on buses throughout the South.

"Tired of Giving In"

Parks is often portrayed as a weary, middle-aged seamstress who was simply too tired to give up her seat, but this is inaccurate. Parks herself would later reflect on the event:

> People always say that I didn't give up my seat because I was tired, but that isn't true. I was not tired physically, or no more tired than I usually was at the end of a working day. I was not old, although some people have an image of me as being old then. I was forty-two. No, the only tired I was, was tired of giving in.[4]

The story of Rosa Parks is not the story of a tired woman—it is the story of a woman who took a courageous stand against injustice. Hers is also a story of a community that felt the same way. Montgomery, Alabama's black citizens in 1955 were simply tired of giving in.

When Rosa Parks refused to give up her seat to a white person, the African American community was ready. Parks was neither the first—nor the last—person to be arrested for violating Montgomery's segregation practices. In her book *Black Women Leaders of the Civil Rights Movement*, Zita Allen writes that "while Parks's courageous decision that December 1 might have been spontaneous, an army of women stood behind her and played a key role in getting the historic Montgomery bus boycott off the ground."[5]

The Montgomery bus boycott was led by extraordinary people. The boycott gave rise to some of the most powerful civil rights leaders in the nation's history, including Martin Luther King Jr. But it is also a story about regular people. Rosa Parks was a seamstress. Martin Luther King was a twenty-six-year-old minister leading his first church. "Courageous leaders like Rosa Parks and Martin Luther King Jr. didn't suddenly appear out of nowhere," writes Marian Wright Edelman in her introduction to a book about the Rosa Parks story. "They weren't superhumans with magical powers. They were ordinary people. . . . But they became heroes and made history because they were willing to stand up and make a difference."[6]

Beyond these leaders, the Montgomery bus boycott is the story of a community coming together in a united effort to protest injustice and to fight for a better future. It is the story of daily sacrifices and struggles made by thousands of people. During the year-long boycott of Montgomery's buses, blacks demonstrated to themselves, to the whites in power, and to the world at large that they could make a difference. The African Americans earned far more than equal treatment on the buses; they earned the self-respect and dignity that whites had been chipping away at for generations.

Chapter One

Life in the Jim Crow South

The story of the Montgomery bus boycott only makes sense if one understands the political, social, and legal context in which the boycott occurred. In Montgomery, Alabama, and throughout the South, racist attitudes had dictated the way people lived since colonial days.

The system of slavery on which the South had been built assumed the black race to be inferior. During slavery, a complex social order was created, based on racist notions that blacks were less intelligent and less capable than whites. On the best plantations, white owners saw themselves as the caretakers of their slaves; in the worst circumstances, slaves were treated no better than dogs.

Following the Civil War—during the period known as Reconstruction—newly freed slaves acted to establish their own churches and institutions, but white lawmakers in southern states responded by passing laws designed to keep power in the hands of whites. Throughout the South, states passed what became known as Jim Crow laws, which mandated that African Americans use separate public facilities from whites. The term

Jim Crow is believed to have originated around 1830 when a white minstrel-show performer blackened his face with charcoal paste and danced while singing "Jump Jim Crow" in the caricature of a silly black person. By the mid-1850s, this had become a common act for minstrel shows, reinforcing racist stereotypes of African Americans. The term *Jim Crow* soon became a racial slur, and by the end of the nineteenth century, government-sanctioned acts of racial discrimination toward African Americans were called Jim Crow laws or practices.

Time did little to change the prevailing attitude among southerners that blacks were inferior. The Declaration of Independence had declared that all men are created equal, but in the South the laws and customs treated blacks as second-class citizens. Over many decades, a culture emerged in which the two races lived separately, coming together only when a white person needed a job done that only a black person would do. In most southern states, blacks and whites lived in separate parts of town and attended different churches and schools. Whites decided that they liked it this way and passed legislation forbidding blacks from using the facilities used by whites. Some states outlawed interracial marriage and even forbade blacks and whites from socializing together.

Plessy v. Ferguson

A number of states also passed laws requiring black train passengers to sit in a separate car. Often, this Jim Crow car had no food service or even bathrooms, making long trips all but impossible.

A black man in shabby clothes represents a Jim Crow minstrel figure in this nineteenth-century illustration.

African Americans realized that the discrimination they faced was unfair and sought protection from the courts. In 1878, they won a minor victory when the Supreme Court ruled that states could not require or enforce segregation on railroads, streetcars, or steamboats that traveled from one state to another, but states continued to enforce Jim Crow laws on travel within the state.

Homer Plessy, a Creole businessman, set out to test an 1890 Louisiana law that segregated railroad cars. Although most of Plessy's ancestors were white, one of his great-grandfathers was black, which made him black in the eyes of the law. The Citizens' Committee, a group of influential African American civic and business leaders, believed that Plessy's light skin and his commitment to civil rights made him an ideal candidate to challenge the segregation law.

On a warm summer day in 1892, Plessy stepped onto the whites-only car of an East Louisiana Railway train in New Orleans headed for Covington, Louisiana. When a porter asked him to move to the car for African Americans, Plessy politely refused. He was arrested and thrown in jail.

When his case came to court, Plessy argued that the law violated his constitutional rights. Specifically, Plessy pointed to the Thirteenth Amendment, which outlawed slavery, and the Fourteenth Amendment, which stated that no state can deny citizens of the United States equal protection of the laws. John Ferguson, the state judge who heard the case, upheld the state's right to make such laws and found Plessy guilty of violating Louisiana's separate car law. He was fined twenty-five dollars.

Plessy took his case all the way to the U.S. Supreme Court. In 1896, the Supreme Court upheld Judge Ferguson's decision by a vote of seven to one. In the majority opinion, Justice Henry Billings Brown wrote: "The object of the amendment was undoubtedly to enforce the absolute equality of the two races before the law, but in the nature of things it could not have been intended to abolish distinctions based upon color, or to enforce social, as distinguished from political equality, or a commingling of the two races upon terms unsatisfactory to either."[7]

Supreme Court Justice John Harlan was the only judge to vote against the decision. In his dissenting opinion, Harlan wrote, "Our Constitution is color-blind, and neither knows nor tolerates

The Louisiana Law for Segregated Railway Cars

Louisiana's laws requiring segregation of railway cars is typical of those passed by southern states in the late 1800s. Below are excerpts from the 1890 law challenged in *Plessy v. Ferguson.*

All railway companies carrying passengers in their coaches in this state [Louisiana], shall provide equal but separate accommodations for the white, and colored races, by providing two or more passenger coaches for each passenger train, or by dividing the passenger coaches by a partition so as to secure separate accommodations: provided, that this section shall not be construed to apply to street railroads. No person or persons shall be permitted to occupy seats in coaches, other than the ones assigned to them, on account of the race they belong to. . . .

The officers of such passenger trains shall have power and are hereby required to assign each passenger to the coach or compartment used for the race to which such passenger belongs; any passenger insisting on going into a coach or compartment to which by race he does not belong, shall be liable to a fine of twenty-five dollars, or in lieu thereof to imprisonment for a period of not more than twenty days in the parish prison . . . ; and should any passenger refuse to occupy the coach or compartment to which he or she is assigned . . . the officer shall have power to refuse to carry such passenger on his train.

Quoted in FindLaw, "U.S. Supreme Court, *Plessy v. Ferguson*." http://caselaw.lp.findlaw.com/scripts/getcase.pl?court=US&vol=163&invol=537.

classes among citizens. In respect of civil rights, all citizens are equal before the law." Harlan also predicted that

the present decision . . . will not only stimulate aggressions, more or less brutal and irritating, upon the admitted rights of colored citizens, but will encourage the belief that it is

possible, by means of state enactments, to defeat the benef-
icent purposes which the people of the United States had in
view when they adopted the recent [the Thirteenth and
Fourteenth] amendments of the Constitution.[8]

Separate but Equal

Plessy v. Ferguson supported the right of states to pass laws segregating the races, as long as facilities were provided for both races.
Although the phrase "separate but equal" was mentioned nowhere in the decision, this became the foundation on which state
and local governments defended their segregation practices.

The Supreme Court's ruling seemed to provide impetus for states to
pass new segregation laws. "Only three states had required or
authorized the Jim Crow waiting room in railway stations before 1899,
but in the next decade nearly all of the other Southern states fell in
line," writes historian C. Vann Woodward. South Carolina passed
legislation segregating first-class train cars in 1898 and extended the
segregation to all cars in 1900. North Carolina segregated its trains in
1899, and Virginia in 1900. Woodward continues:

> Street cars had been common in Southern cities since the
> 'eighties, but only Georgia had a segregation law applying
> to them before the end of the century. Then in quick suc-
> cession North Carolina and Virginia adopted such a law in
> 1901, Louisiana in 1902, Arkansas, South Carolina, and
> Tennessee in 1903, Mississippi and Maryland in 1904,
> Florida in 1905, and Oklahoma in 1907. . . . [A] Mont-
> gomery city ordinance of 1906 was the first to require a
> completely separate Jim Crow street car. During these years
> the older seaboard states of the South also extended the
> segregation laws to steamboats.[9]

States soon passed laws requiring segregation in other facilities
as well. Georgia passed a law mandating separate parks for blacks
and whites; Louisiana passed legislation requiring separate entrances, exits, ticket windows, and ticket sellers at circus and tent
shows. The city of Birmingham applied the principle to "any
room, hall, theatre, picture house, auditorium, yard, court, ball
park, or other indoor or outdoor place" and specified that the
races be separated "by well defined physical barriers."[10]

Woodward writes: "Up and down the avenues and byways of Southern life appeared with an increasing profusion the little signs: 'Whites Only' or 'Colored.' . . . Many appeared without requirement by law—over entrances and exits, at theaters and boarding houses, toilets and water fountains, waiting rooms and ticket windows."[11]

Workplaces also were segregated. In addition to separate workrooms, some states passed laws forbidding blacks and whites to use the same doorways, stairways, or pay windows at the same time. A South Carolina law even dictated that blacks and whites had to look out of different windows during their breaks.

Jim Crow also made its way into northern cities, accompanying the large numbers of African Americans who moved there. In a three-year span from 1916 to 1919, over half a million blacks fled the South; 1 million more followed in the 1920s. During the

Segregation was so widespread that blacks even had to use separate drinking fountains.

Great Depression, black sharecroppers joined relatives and friends in Chicago, Detroit, New York, and other cities. Discrimination and racism soon followed.

Segregation even spread to the federal government. During his 1912 campaign for president, Woodrow Wilson promised "to see justice done to the colored people in every matter."[12] Within a year of his election, he had issued an executive order requiring segregation in federal workplaces, restrooms, and cafeterias.

A Disenfranchised People

African Americans had little power to change the laws. Throughout the South, blacks were denied the right to vote. One method that southern states used was the poll tax. This was a fee that a person had to pay to vote. By 1904, all eleven southern states that had formed the Confederacy during the Civil War had made payment of a poll tax a voting prerequisite. Since newly freed slaves had little or no money, the tax prohibited all but a very few from

African American protesters demand voting rights. Throughout the South blacks had to pay poll taxes or take literacy tests before being allowed to vote.

voting. It was, in the opinion of one observer at the time, "the most effective bar to Negro suffrage ever devised."[13]

Literacy tests were another tactic by which whites denied blacks the right to vote. Some of these tests required those wishing to register to recite the entire Constitution or to answer questions about state laws. Even if a black person could pass the literacy tests, the white evaluator would often say they had failed. To ensure that whites would not be disenfranchised by such laws, states enacted grandfather clauses, which gave the right to vote to anyone whose grandfather had been eligible to vote. Since the grandfathers of most African Americans were slaves, they were rarely grandfathered in.

Measures to keep blacks from voting persisted well into the twentieth century. As late as the 1960s, Dallas County, Alabama, required African Americans registering to vote to pass an oral examination about the U.S. Constitution. They also had to possess "good character"—a term that the white registrants could define as they saw fit. Although more than half of the people living in Dallas County were black, these measures ensured that the voter rolls included only 1 percent of black residents.

Southern states also excluded black participation through primary elections. Beginning with Mississippi in 1902, states passed laws declaring political parties to be private organizations. This meant that the protections granted by the Fifteenth Amendment, which said that "governments in the United States may not prevent a citizen from voting because of his race, color, or previous condition of servitude," would not apply to party activities, such as the primaries in which candidates were chosen. Declaring political parties to be private organizations enabled leaders to establish different voting rules, and they quickly used this authority to say that only whites could vote. The white primary prevented the small number of blacks who succeeded in registering to vote from having any say in who would run for office.

As if this were not enough to bar blacks from voting, whites engaged in intimidation tactics. African Americans knew that they could lose their job or be evicted from their homes if they tried to register to vote. In some cities, whites lined the streets to the polls on election day, blocking the path of African Americans and hurling abuse at those who attempted to pass by. When all else failed, the Ku Klux Klan and other groups threatened—and carried out—violence. Blacks who persisted in trying to vote were beaten or even killed. Historian Woodward concludes, "By one means or another, including intimidation and terror, Negroes were effectively prevented from registering even when they had the courage to try."[14] E.D. Nixon, who worked to register fellow African Americans, later told a newspaper reporter that the whites of Montgomery were effective in "keeping the Negro afraid and also keeping him unlearned."[15]

The Social Order

Violence was a powerful tool for enforcing Jim Crow laws. More than five thousand African Americans were lynched between 1882 and 1936. Lynching was not reserved for those who were guilty of an offense; it was used as a deterrent for almost any behavior that whites did not like. Not surprisingly, few blacks would stand up to discriminatory practices when it might bring down the wrath of the white mob on one's parents, spouse, or children.

Although most blacks were hauled off under the cover of darkness, some lynchings became public spectacles, carried out with the support of the white community. The gangs of whites involved in such violence were rarely caught or brought to trial. The few that were tried were almost never convicted. Grace Hale, who studied the culture of segregation in the South in the early twentieth century, writes:

> It was a world where people who went to church some days watched or participated in the torture of their neighbors on others. . . . Lynchers drove cars, spectators used cameras, out-of-town visitors arrived on specially chartered excursion trains, and the towns and counties in which these horrifying events happened had newspapers, telegraph offices, and even radio stations that announced times and locations of these upcoming violent spectacles.[16]

Blacks were also at the mercy of local law enforcement and other authorities. Employers could fire blacks at any time and could—and did—use this power to keep blacks from voting or otherwise gaining power. Bus drivers, restaurant owners, theater

People take part in a reenactment of a 1946 lynching at Moore's Ford Bridge in Monroe, Georgia.

ushers, and other whites had authority to refuse to serve African Americans without reason. An African American who argued, even politely, risked being beaten before being arrested for disorderly behavior. Woodward explains, "The Jim Crow laws put the authority of the state or city in the voice of the street-car conductor, the railway brakeman, the bus driver, the theater usher, and also into the voice of the hoodlum of the public parks and playgrounds."[17]

The Myth of Separate but Equal

In *Plessy v. Ferguson*, the Supreme Court held that segregating facilities was legal as long as they were of equal quality. In reality, however, rarely were services or facilities for blacks as nice as those that were reserved for whites. African Americans had to live with unsanitary public bathrooms, broken drinking-water fountains, and uncomfortable seats on buses and in train stations. In the prologue to *The Eyes on the Prize Civil Rights Reader*, Vincent Harding writes of the "harsh and often immovable" reality of Jim Crow laws:

Wherever black people traveled or lived in the South, and in too many parts of the North, they were faced with the humiliation of seeing doors that were open to white citizens legally

An Inside Look at Jim Crow

Mahalia Jackson, a world-renowned gospel singer, writes of her experiences with discrimination while on a concert tour of the South in the 1960s:

There were lots of white people at [my] concerts and they sat side by side with colored folks. . . . Those white people . . . applauded just as hard as anybody . . . and afterward some of them came around to tell me how much they had enjoyed the evening.

But the minute I left the concert hall I felt as if I had stepped back into the jungle. . . . There was no place for us to eat or sleep on the main highways. Restaurants wouldn't serve us. Teen-age white girls who were serving as carhops would come bouncing out to the car and stop dead when they saw we were Negroes, spin around without a word and walk away. Some gasoline stations didn't want to sell us gas and oil. Some told us that no restrooms were available. The looks of anger at the sight of us colored folks sitting in a nice car were frightening to see. . . .

When the white people came crowding around us after the concerts—ministers, teachers, educated people—I thanked them for their praise but I felt like saying, "How big does a person have to grow down in this part of the country before he's going to stand up and say, 'Let us stop treating other men and women and children with such cruelty just because they are born colored!'"

Quoted in Gerda Lerner, ed., *Black Women in White America: A Documentary History*. New York: Vintage, 1972, pp. 383–84.

A Greyhound bus station in Louisville, Kentucky, maintained a separate outhouse (shown in a 1943 photo) for black riders.

closed to them: restaurant and motel doors, movie house doors, skilled employment doors, Marine Corps and Air Force doors, the large doors to public parks, pools, beaches, entire neighborhoods, the doors to public service were all closed. Or they would find two sets of doors, two kinds of facilities, from ticket line to water fountains, from waiting rooms to public schools. One white, one colored, one reasonably clean, well cared for, well supplied, the other usually broken, neglected by the white authorities, shamefully unequal.[18]

Ralph D. Abernathy, a Montgomery minister who was among the most vocal opponents of Jim Crow laws, recalls that even when there was a restroom for black people, there would be only one for both women and men. "And the janitor never would clean up the restroom for the colored people,"[19] he adds.

Getting an education was all but impossible for African Americans. Schools for black children often had no heat, no running water, and few books or supplies. Black children were taught by teachers who had little education themselves. Blacks also attended school for fewer days than whites. The school that Rosa Parks attended in her hometown of Pine Level, Alabama, for example, was open only six months a year, while white children went to school for nine months a year. Montgomery, like many communities in the South, did not have a high school for African Americans until the 1950s.

With little education, it was far more difficult for African Americans to get jobs than whites. By denying blacks membership, trade unions further restricted the opportunities afforded to blacks. Abernathy writes that in the 1950s,

> Blacks were permitted to hold only the menial jobs, domestic workers and common and ordinary laborers. The only professional jobs that were open to blacks were the field of pastoring a black church and the schoolteaching profession, which was open because of segregated schools. . . . We were the last to be hired and the first to be fired.[20]

Separate but Equal on Montgomery's Buses

In 1945, Alabama passed a law requiring that all bus companies under its jurisdiction enforce segregation laws that dictated where—and even if—African Americans could sit on the buses. The front ten rows (twenty of the total thirty-six seats) were reserved for whites. Even if there were no whites on the bus, African American riders were not allowed to sit in the white section; if all sixteen seats in the black section were taken, African American riders had to stand. Because an estimated 75 to 85 percent of riders on Montgomery buses were black, it was not unusual to see a bus with blacks crowded in the aisle standing over rows of empty seats.

The line between the white and black sections of the bus was not fixed. The driver had the power to expand the seating for whites into the black section by ordering blacks to relinquish their seats. The law forbade African Americans from sitting in the same row as whites, so the driver typically ordered the entire row of blacks to move to accommodate a white passenger who did not have a seat. Rosa Parks later recalled, "Having to take a certain section [on a bus] because of your race was humiliating, but having to stand up because a particular driver wanted to keep a white person from having to stand was, to my mind, most inhumane."[21]

According to the rules of Montgomery's bus companies, blacks had to enter the bus through the front door, put their money in the coin box, then get off and walk back to enter through the rear door to take their seat in the back of the bus. White bus drivers sometimes drove off before black passengers who had paid could reenter. This was among the many ways drivers misused their authority over black riders. Zita Allen writes,

> Many drivers frequently went out of their way to humiliate, berate, demean, and dehumanize their black passengers. Some operators snatched transfers from the hands of black passengers, or threw transfers or change in coins at them. Some refused to make change for blacks and accepted only exact fares. On rainy days black riders were "passed by" because white passengers did not want them standing over them.[22]

White and black bus riders sit in different parts of a bus.

Resigned to the Jim Crow system, Montgomery's blacks over-looked these humiliations and the discriminatory practices of the bus companies. "Intermittently, twenty to twenty-five thousand black people in Montgomery rode city buses," Jo Ann Robinson later wrote, "and I would estimate that, up until the boycott of December 5, 1955, about three out of five had suffered some un-happy experience on the public transit lines."[23] Robinson further described the plight of black riders:

Black riders would often forget pride and feeling, forget the terribly offensive names they were so often called when they dared to sit in one of the ten reserved seats. Hurting feet, tired bodies, empty stomachs often tempted them to sit down. [But derogatory names] brought them to their feet again. When sheer exhaustion or tired, aching limbs forced them to forget pride and feeling, they sat down, sometimes for one minute, maybe two. Even a minute's rest helped some. But they would rise again, either in tears, or retaliat-ing curses hurled at them at the driver. Whatever the case was, they would be badly shaken, nervous, tired, fearful, and angry.[24]

Beyond humiliation, there was violence. In 1950, Thomas Ed-ward Brooks, a twenty-year-old soldier who was born in Mont-gomery, was beaten with a billy club, dragged off the bus, and then shot and killed by a Montgomery police officer after he re-fused to follow the bus driver's instructions to get off the bus by the front door and back on at the back. Mattie Johnson, who wit-nessed the event from her seat on the back of the bus, recalled later, "There never was nothing done about the shooting, al-though it was a pure cold-blood hate killing. The police swept it under the rug, like they did a lot of other things back then. Said it was 'self-defense,' when anybody coulda seen the boy was shot in the back like he was a mad dog or something."[25] Of course, not all of the bus drivers were cruel, but the vio-lence that occurred on that day in 1950 was not an anomaly. In addition to Brooks, at least two other African Americans were killed on Montgomery's buses over the next three years. As secre-tary of the Montgomery branch of the NAACP, Rosa Parks knew of many cases in which African Americans were mistreated. Parks

Jo Ann Robinson Remembers

◼

One of the reasons that the Montgomery bus boycott was so successful was because many African American men and women had had bad experiences on city buses. In this excerpt, Jo Ann Robinson writes of how she inadvertently sat in a white section of the bus. Her thoughts of visiting her family and friends were interrupted by an angry bus driver.

From the far distance of my reverie I thought I heard . . . an unpleasant voice, but I was too happy to worry about voices, or any noise for that matter. But the same words were repeated, in a stronger, unsavory tone, and I opened my eyes. . . . The bus driver had stopped the bus, turned in his seat, and was speaking to me!

"If you can sit in the fifth row from the front of the other buses in Montgomery, suppose you get off and ride in one of them!" I heard him, but the message did not register with me. . . . I had not even noticed that the bus had come to a full stop.

Suddenly the driver left his seat and stood over me. His hand was drawn back as if he were going to strike me. "Get up from there!" he yelled. He repeated it, for, dazed, I had not moved. "Get up from there!"

I leaped to my feet, afraid he would hit me, and ran to the front door to get off the bus. . . . Tears were falling rapidly from my eyes. It suddenly occurred to me that I was supposed to go to the back door to get off, not the front! However, I was too upset, frightened and tearful to move.

Quoted in Jo Ann Gibson Robinson, *The Montgomery Bus Boycott and the Women Who Started It: The Memoir of Jo Ann Gibson Robinson.* Knoxville: University of Tennessee Press, 1987, p. 17.

later wrote that "nothing came out of" many of the cases that had come to the attention of the NAACP "because the person that was abused would be too intimidated to sign an affidavit, or to make a statement."[26]

It is not surprising that few blacks stood up to the discrimination they faced daily. A simple act of defiance like that taken by Rosa Parks often came at great cost. But there were always a courageous few who, for one reason or another, tested Jim Crow laws. From their examples, others drew strength. On their shoulders rested the civil rights movement.

Chapter Two

Seeds of Resistance

Over the decades following the Civil War, blacks and whites became accustomed to the complex rules of segregation. By the mid-1950s, blacks and whites attended different schools, churches, theaters, restaurants, and even public parks. Even under Jim Crow, blacks and whites rode the same buses, however. While there was a set of strict rules governing the behavior of African Americans, confrontations were not uncommon. Occasionally, an African American rider stood up to the system of injustice. Sometimes, the rider was evicted from the bus, arrested, or fined. Always, there was an underlying threat of violence.

Sometimes confrontations arose from a simple problem or inconvenience. An African American might be arrested and fined for "talking back" to a driver who scolded her for not having correct change or who refused to provide the correct transfer. In other cases, problems arose because riders were unaware of the rules governing their conduct. This is what happened when Edwina and Marshall Johnson boarded a city bus in Montgomery in 1949. Just ten and twelve years old, the siblings from New Jersey were visiting relatives in Montgomery. Unaware of the segregation laws, the children refused to give up their seats to a white man and boy. Edwina and Marshall were arrested and held in jail for two days before being convicted of violating the city's segregation laws. The judge threatened to send them to reform school, but the attorney hired by their relatives convinced the judge to issue a fine and send the children back to New Jersey.

Fighting the System

Throughout the country, blacks fought for justice. It was often easier for those in the North to speak out against injustice, and speak out they did. W.E.B. DuBois, an African American scholar, also took up the crusade against discrimination and racism. "By every civilized peaceful method we must strive for the rights which the world accords man,"[27] he said. In 1906, he and other like-minded citizens joined together in the Niagara Movement to advocate civil justice and abolish racial discrimination.

Following a race riot that broke out in Springfield, Illinois, in the summer of 1908, several black and white leaders came to-

W.E.B. DuBois (left) meets with other members of the Niagara Movement in West Virginia in 1906.

gether in New York to discuss proposals for an organization that would advocate the civil and political rights of African Americans. One of the founders later explained that the group "wanted to do something at once that should move the country" and decided to issue a call for a national conference to "discover the beginnings, at least, of a 'large and powerful body of citizens' . . . engaged in religious, social and educational work."[28]

The result of this call—the National Negro Conference—was held in New York on May 31 and June 1, 1909. The platform signed at this meeting concluded:

As first and immediate steps toward remedying these national wrongs, so full of peril for the whites as well as the blacks, we demand of Congress and the Executive:

(1) That the Constitution be strictly enforced and the civil rights guaranteed under the Fourteenth Amendment be secured impartially to all,

(2) That there be equal educational opportunities for all and in all the States, and that public school expenditure be the same for the Negro and white child,

(3) That in accordance with the Fifteenth Amendment the right of the Negro to the ballot on the same terms as other citizens be recognized in every part of the country.[29]

At the second annual meeting, May 12, 1910, the committee adopted the formal name of the organization—the National Association for the Advancement of Colored People (NAACP).

In 1910, in the face of intense adversity, the NAACP began its legacy of fighting legal battles addressing social injustice. Its first defendant was Pink Franklin, a black sharecropper who had killed a policeman when two armed policemen broke into his home in the middle of the night without stating their purpose to arrest him on a civil charge. Although this was a clear case of self-defense, Franklin was convicted of murder and sentenced to death. The NAACP succeeded in changing his sentence to life in prison. (Franklin was set free in 1919.)

The NAACP also launched a campaign against the lynchings that were all too common in the South. Since southerners seemed to do little or nothing to put a stop to these horrors, the NAACP

The NAACP

The National Association for the Advancement of Colored People (NAACP) was founded on February 12, 1909, by a diverse and multiracial group of civil rights advocates. Prompted in part by race riots that had occurred in Springfield, Illinois, in the summer of 1908, the NAACP was formed to address the challenges facing people of color.

The NAACP worked for several decades to overturn Jim Crow laws and reverse the separate but equal doctrine ushered in by the Supreme Court's decision in *Plessy v. Ferguson*. NAACP lawyers won a major victory in 1954 when the Supreme Court ruled in *Brown v. Board of Education* that the segregation of elementary schools was unconstitutional. Bolstered by that victory, the NAACP pushed for desegregation of other public facilities throughout the South.

Leaders of NAACP's Montgomery chapter played a critical role in the Montgomery bus boycott. When the local chapter refused to provide a list of its members, out of fear of retaliation, the state of Alabama responded by barring the NAACP from operating within its borders.

The NAACP continues to advocate for civil rights and to fight against discriminatory practices in the courts.

sought a federal lynching law that would outlaw the practice throughout the country. Although the NAACP failed to convince Congress to pass legislation, the group persuaded President Wilson and other politicians to condemn the practice.

Much of the NAACP's efforts focused on securing the rights guaranteed by the Fourteenth and Fifteenth Amendments by overturning Jim Crow laws. The NAACP achieved its first major success in *Buchanan v. Worley*, a 1917 case in which the Supreme Court declared unconstitutional a Louisville, Kentucky, ordinance allowing people to sell their houses only to whites. The NAACP also focused on voting rights. In 1915, the Supreme Court outlawed the use of grandfather clauses in voting legislation, and in 1927, the all-white primary was eliminated.

African Americans joined together in other organizations to fight the system. Through organizations like the Montgomery Voters' League, which was founded by E.D. Nixon in 1940, activists helped African Americans register to vote. Nixon himself led groups of blacks to the courthouse to register. "More than once he was turned away at the door by city police officers or sheriff's deputies," writes Donnie Williams in *The Thunder of Angels*. "He was warned again and again that he would be arrested if he didn't stop leading people to the registrar's office. But he didn't stop."[30]

As a member of the Brotherhood of Sleeping Car Porters, one of the few unions with African American members, Nixon also used his union ties to eliminate discrimination. On his trips to New York, Nixon saw firsthand a world in which blacks and whites traveled on the same train cars and ate in the same cafeterias. Nixon began to demand these same privileges in the South:

> At Union Station in Montgomery, blacks could not use the water fountains. They had to go into the Colored Only bathrooms, bend down, and fold their hands to cup water

African American railroad porters relax at the Harlem, New York, headquarters of the Brotherhood of Sleeping Car Porters.

from the faucet. After Nixon argued the point in the late 1930s, management installed electric water fountains for blacks. At the large Sears, Roebuck and Company store there were no bathroom facilities for blacks. Once again, Nixon confronted the management and pointed out the problem. The management acquiesced and installed toilets for blacks.[31]

World War II Ushers in Changes

Life in America was changed by World War II. During the war, many black Americans fought side by side with white comrades. Unfortunately, the heroism of blacks was often overlooked because of the deeply entrenched prejudices of Americans, but African Americans repeatedly demonstrated bravery on and off the battlefield.

When they returned home, many black servicemen were ready to fight for equal rights. "The black man . . . plods wearily no longer—he is striding Freedom Road," wrote Adam Clayton Powell Jr. in a 1945 book. "He is ready to throw himself into the struggle to make the dream of America become flesh and blood, bread and butter, freedom and equality."[32]

In the years following the war, African Americans won a series of judgments in their favor. In 1945, Connecticut became the first state to ban Jim Crow laws. Just three years later, President Harry S. Truman issued an executive order ending segregation in the armed forces. White primaries and literacy tests were declared unconstitutional. And a number of colleges and universities opened their doors to blacks for the first time.

Brown v. Board of Education

The most critical success of civil rights activists was *Brown v. Board of Education of Topeka Kansas*, a landmark case heard by the Supreme Court in 1954. The case was filed by NAACP lawyers on behalf of thirteen black families that were denied enrollment in the closest school because of their race. (Oliver Brown, a minister, was the first parent listed in the suit, so the case was named after him.) When the U.S. District Court in Kansas ruled against the plaintiffs, the NAACP appealed to the Supreme Court.

The NAACP had pleaded similar cases in other states. Cases in Delaware, the District of Columbia, Virginia, and South Carolina were also waiting to be heard by the Supreme Court. The Court

A Post-War Call for Action

———◼———

Blacks returned home from World War I prepared to fight for their freedom. In this editorial from the May 1919 *Crisis* magazine, W.E.B. DuBois called for action.

> By the God of Heaven, we are cowards and jackasses if now that the war is over, we do not marshal every ounce of our brain and brawn to fight the forces of hell in our own land.
>
> We return.
> We return from fighting.
> We return fighting!
> Make way for Democracy! We saved it in France, and by the great Jehovah, we will save it in the United States of America, or know the reason why.

Quoted in Gerald C. Hynes, "A Biographical Sketch of W.E.B. DuBois," W.E.B. DuBois Learning Center. www.duboislc.org/html/DuBoisBio.html.

decided to rule on these cases together because although they were "premised on different facts and different local conditions," they had "a common legal question." The Court further outlined the plaintiffs' claims:

> In each of the cases, minors of the Negro race, through their legal representatives, seek the aid of the courts in obtaining admission to the public schools of their community on a non-segregated basis. In each instance, they had been denied admission to schools attended by white children under laws requiring or permitting segregation according to race. This segregation was alleged to deprive the plaintiffs of the equal protection of the laws under the Fourteenth Amendment.[33]

Unlike the lower courts, the Supreme Court found that the rights of plaintiffs to equal education had been denied. In the majority opinion, Chief Justice Earl Warren wrote: "We conclude

The young plaintiffs in *Brown v. Board of Education* are seated in front of their parents in this portrait taken in 1953.

that in the field of public education, the doctrine of 'separate but equal' has no place. Separate educational facilities are inherently unequal."[34]

The reaction among the black community was immediate. Reflecting on how he felt upon hearing the Supreme Court's decision, a black Marine later wrote:

> Elation took hold of me so strongly that I found it very difficult to refrain from yielding to an urge of jubilation. . . . I felt that at last the government was willing to assert itself on behalf of first-class citizenship, even for Negroes. I experienced a sense of loyalty that I had never felt before. I was sure that this was the beginning of a new era.[35]

Defiance and Militancy

Not everyone was satisfied with the slow pace of change brought about by the courts, however. Some African Americans took a more militant stance in demanding justice. Among them was Vernon Johns, who served as a pastor at the Court Street Baptist Church in Montgomery, Alabama, during the 1920s. Johns spoke out against segregation in his sermons and talked about its economic, social, and political costs to the African American community. He refused to abide by segregation laws. He and his family refused to attend segregated movie theaters or restaurants. Throughout the 1940s and 1950s, Johns attempted to lead Montgomery's African Americans in resisting Jim Crow laws. Most blacks found his approaches too confrontational. "Reverend Johns refused to be pushed back at any place, and he was very vehement with whites," said a parishioner of his church. "He used to block doors, he used to stand on corners and sort of bless them out."[36]

Others resisted in less confrontational ways. Author Kai Friese describes how the NAACP youth group in Montgomery expressed their opposition to Jim Crow:

> The members of the youth group often went into white libraries and tried to borrow books. Sometimes they made a point of sitting in the white section of segregated restaurants or buses. They would almost always be chased away by the librarians, managers, and drivers. But they were making it clear to everyone that they didn't want to live in a segregated world.[37]

Collective Action

African Americans also came together to protest racist practices on buses and railroads. In 1953, for instance, the African American community in Baton Rouge, Louisiana, staged a boycott of city buses. This was by no means the first time blacks had boycotted transportation services—in the late 1800s, blacks boycotted streetcar lines in twenty-seven cities—but it demonstrated anew

A sign mounted above a theater around 1950 clearly marks the entrance to be used by black patrons.

that a boycott could be an effective weapon against unfair practices.

In Baton Rouge, an estimated 80 percent of the riders were black. The city passed a law allowing whites to take seats from the front toward the rear and blacks to fill the seats starting in the rear and moving forward, but the state declared that the city ordinance was unconstitutional because the state law required buses to be segregated, with the first ten rows reserved for whites. Leaders of the African American community fought back by asking blacks to stay off city buses. Within a week, the buses were virtually empty.

During the boycott, Baton Rouge's black leaders held mass meetings at a church each evening to communicate the vision and connect with the black community. Thousands of blacks attended the meetings, which became important rallying points for the community. Money collected at the rallies was used to help pay for gas to drive black residents to and from their jobs.

Two weeks after the boycott was staged, Baton Rouge's white leaders met with the leaders of the boycott to hammer out a solution. The compromise kept intact the spirit of the previous city ordinance—blacks would sit from the back forward and whites from the front toward the back until all seats were taken. The black community agreed to the compromise and ended the boycott.

The effects of the Baton Rouge bus boycott went beyond the new policies on the city's buses. By proving that Jim Crow laws could be successfully challenged by mass action, the boycott set the stage for future protests.

A Boycott Is Threatened

The potential power of a bus boycott did not go unnoticed in Montgomery. Over the years, the Women's Political Council (WPC), a local civic organization for African American women founded in 1946, had received countless complaints from blacks who had been mistreated on city buses. Jo Ann Robinson, the president of the WPC, made ending segregation on the buses a top priority. In May 1954, Robinson wrote a letter to Mayor W.A. Gayle on behalf of the WPC hinting at the possibility of a bus boycott:

More and more of our people are already arranging with neighbors and friends to ride to keep from being insulted and humiliated by bus drivers. There has been talk from twenty-five or more local organizations of planning a city-wide boycott of busses. We, sir, do not feel that forceful measures are necessary in bargaining for a convenience which is right for all bus passengers.[38]

Robinson stopped short of demanding an end to segregation. Rather, she asked the city to make more seats available for blacks. She also suggested that the bus company change the policy whereby blacks had to pay at the front of the bus and then go around to the rear, put additional bus stops in black residential sections of town, and hire black drivers. Above all, she requested better treatment for black passengers.

The Search for a Test Case

As the WPC was threatening a bus boycott, NAACP leaders were looking for an opportunity to test the segregation laws in the courts. There were plenty of blacks who had been the victims of racial discrimination, but the NAACP needed someone who could earn the respect of both blacks and whites and who would be able to deal with the publicity that would result from being at the center of a bus boycott—as well as the threats of violence that would almost certainly result.

On March 2, 1955, the local NAACP thought it had found whom it was looking for in Claudette Colvin.

Colvin, an African American teenager, was sitting near the rear door of a Montgomery bus when the driver told her and her fellow passengers to get up to give their seats to white passengers. Everyone did as they were told except Colvin. She refused even after police arrived. As the police dragged her off the bus in handcuffs, she continued to assert that she had a constitutional right to ride the bus because she had paid the fare.

In fact, Colvin had not violated any segregation laws. She was not sitting in the seats reserved for whites. The law required blacks to relinquish their seats only if there were available seats further toward the rear of the bus. Although this was the official policy, in practice, drivers typically ordered blacks to give up their seats to white riders even if that meant standing in the aisle.

Colvin was no troublemaker. She was quiet, well mannered, deeply religious, and an A student at Montgomery's black high school. Colvin later explained that her actions were prompted in part by what she had learned about Jim Crow and the Constitution in school and as a member of the NAACP youth council.

Fred Gray, one of just two black lawyers in Montgomery, agreed to represent Colvin. Gray discussed options with others in the community, including E.D. Nixon and Clifford Durr, a local white attorney who supported blacks in their fight for equality. In the end, they decided to meet with the leaders of the city and the bus company to ask for leniency for Colvin. The meetings were fruitless. Colvin was convicted not only of violating the city's segregation laws, but also of resisting arrest.

Colvin's defenders were furious. They now saw the Colvin case as a missed opportunity to contest segregation laws—a mistake that they vowed not to repeat. "Claudette gave to all of us the moral courage to do what we later did," Gray wrote later. "[She] had more courage, in my opinion than any of the persons involved in the movement."[39]

The Time Had Come

Just a few months later, another NAACP member refused to move when the bus driver asked her to. This time, the African American community was prepared.

Rosa Parks had much in common with Claudette Colvin —including the fundamental belief that it was time for blacks to demand their constitutional rights. But she was older and more mature than Colvin. Parks had been one of the first women

In 2005, Claudette Colvin marked the anniversary of her 1955 challenge of segregated seating laws in Montgomery, Alabama.

Rosa Parks's Childhood

—————◼—————

Rosa Louise McCauley was born in Tuskegee, Alabama, on February 4, 1913. Her father, James McCauley, was a carpenter; her mother, Leona Edwards, was a teacher. Rosa's father abandoned the family when Rosa was a baby, and when Rosa was two, she moved with her brother Sylvester and their mother to her grandparents' farm in Pine Level, Alabama.

Many African American children received little schooling, but Rosa's mother believed that education was important. At age eleven, Rosa was enrolled in the Montgomery Industrial School for Girls, a private school for black children run by northerners. She had to leave after five years to care for her sick mother and grandmother, but she was intent on returning to school as soon as she could and, in 1934, became one of the few black girls in Montgomery to receive a high school diploma.

Rosa was a good student and a quiet girl, but her later demonstration of defiance did not surprise those who knew her as a child. In her autobiography, Rosa wrote of her early recollections of the racist society in which she grew up. She remembered being frightened by the Ku Klux Klan and lynchings. She also recalled watching her grandfather sit up with a shotgun as the Klan marched in front of her house. She also wrote of her nightmares in which the house caught on fire from a cross burning on the front lawn. These experiences may have crystallized Rosa's commitment to creating a better life for her fellow African Americans.

Rosa McCauley married Raymond Parks in 1932. Raymond had fought to obtain justice for the Scottsboro boys, who had been wrongfully accused of rape. He and Rosa joined the local NAACP, where Rosa would continue her role fighting for civil rights for many years.

in Montgomery to join the NAACP and had served as its secretary for twelve years, which had brought her into close contact with Nixon and other local African American leaders.

Parks was also friends with Fred Gray. She often helped Gray with work in his office and talked about his cases over lunch. She knew about Claudette Colvin and the many others who had been arrested on city buses and convicted of violating Jim Crow laws.

Many researchers believe it was Parks's experience at the Highlander Folk School that cemented her commitment to undoing segregation policies. In the summer of 1955, Parks attended a program to discuss the desegregation of schools following the *Brown v. Board of Education* ruling. "Highlander was known throughout the South as a radical educational center that was overtly planning for the total desegregation of the South," writes

Following the eventual success of the boycott, Rosa Parks rides in the front of a bus in Montgomery, Alabama.

author Herbert Kohl. "Rosa Parks was aware of that [and] indicated that she intended to become an active participant in other attempts to break down the barriers of segregation."[40]

Parks's husband, Raymond, also had a history of civil rights activism. In the 1930s, when he and Rosa were newlyweds, he had worked to help free the Scottsboro boys, black youths falsely accused of rape. Early in their marriage, the young Rosa Parks saw her home used for secret meetings at which her husband and others discussed how they might win justice for the boys.

Rosa Parks demonstrated what she had learned from leaders of the civil rights movement in a simple act of defiance. When Parks refused to give up her seat on the bus, she did not plan to start a boycott. She did not plan to become a test case for the NAACP. "I didn't get on the bus with the intention of being arrested, I got on the bus with the intention of going home." Rosa Parks later explained. "The time had just come when I had been pushed as far as I could stand to be pushed."[41]

Chapter Three

The Boycott Begins

O n December 1, 1955, Rosa Parks was arrested for violating Montgomery's segregation laws. A police officer led her off the bus and took her to the police station, where she was booked and put in a jail cell. Parks's initial requests to use the telephone were denied, but eventually a matron came to the cell to escort Parks to a phone booth. "She gave me a card and told me to write down who I was calling and the telephone number," Parks recalls. "She placed a dime in the slot, dialed the number, and stayed close by to hear what I was saying."[42]

Parks's mother answered the phone. The first thing she asked her daughter was whether she had been beaten. Parks answered no, then asked her mother to send her husband to get her out of jail.

Like most African Americans in Montgomery, Raymond Parks did not have a car, so he began to call friends for a ride. He also needed to borrow money so that he could post bail for Rosa.

Word traveled quickly. When E.D. Nixon heard that Parks had been arrested, he tried to reach Fred Gray, but he was not home. Nixon then telephoned Clifford Durr, who, with his wife, Virginia, agreed to help Nixon bail Parks out of jail.

When Parks arrived home, a small crowd gathered to discuss the day's events. "Everyone was angry about what had happened to me and talking about how it should never happen again," writes Parks. "I knew that I would never, never ride another seg-regated bus, even if I had to walk to work."[43]

Nixon asked Parks if she would be willing to allow her expe-rience to test the legality of segregation laws. Park's husband and mother were concerned about her safety; they all knew that whites did not take kindly to those who opposed the Jim Crow system. Virginia Durr remembered Raymond Parks being partic-ularly reluctant: "He kept saying over and over again, 'Rosa, the white folks will kill you.'"[44]

Accounts disagree about whether Rosa Parks was reluctant ini-tially, but she quickly put aside whatever concerns she had about participating. She had been committed to the civil rights movement

Rosa Parks arrives at the courthouse in 1956 for her trial on charges of refusing to move to the segregated section of a city bus.

for a long time. She had heard many complaints from victims of racism. She believed it was time for her to take a stand.

Nixon was elated. He had worked with Parks for many years and believed that she was the perfect person for a test case. The whites who opposed segregation would have a hard time finding anything to criticize in Parks's background. "She was honest, she was clean, she had integrity,"[45] Nixon later wrote. Nixon was not alone in this opinion. Johnnie Carr, a lifelong friend of Rosa Parks, later wrote that Parks "was very quiet and always stayed out of trouble. But whatever she did, she always put herself completely into it."[46]

News Spreads

When Fred Gray heard that Parks had been arrested, he immediately called Jo Ann Robinson. He knew that the WPC had been considering a bus boycott for years. "If you have ever planned to do anything with the council, now is your time,"[47] Gray told Robinson. Robinson called the officers of the WPC's three chapters and "as many of the men who had supported us as I could reach," she recalled later. When she told them that Rosa Parks had been arrested, they responded, "You have the plans, put them into operation."[48]

On the night of December 1, Robinson stayed up all night. She wrote a flyer calling for a boycott. It read:

Another Negro woman has been arrested and thrown in jail because she refused to get up out of her seat on the bus for a white person to sit down. It is the second time since the Claudette Colvin case that a Negro woman has been arrested for the same thing. This has to be stopped. Negroes have rights, too, for if Negroes did not ride the buses, they could not operate. Three-fourths of the riders are Negroes, yet we are arrested, or have to stand over empty seats. If we do not do something to stop these arrests, they will continue. The next time it may be you, or your daughter, or mother. This woman's case will come up on Monday. We are, therefore, asking every Negro to stay off the buses Monday in protest of the arrest and trial. Don't ride the buses to work, to town, to school, or anywhere on Monday. You can afford to stay out of school for one day if you have

In Her Own Words

In this autobiographical account, Rosa Parks writes that she took the bus as usual on December 1, 1955, and describes what happened next.

The [whites who got on at the stop] filled up the white seats, and one man was left standing. The driver looked back and noticed the man standing. Then he looked back at us. He said, "Let me have those front seats," because they were the front seats of the black section. Didn't anybody move. We just sat right where we were, the four of us. Then he spoke a second time: "Y'all better make it light on yourselves and let me have those seats."

The man in the window seat next to me stood up, and I moved to let him pass by me, and then I looked across the aisle and saw that the two women were also standing. I moved over to the window seat. I could not see how standing up was going to "make it light" for me. The more we gave in and complied, the worse they treated us. . . .

People always say that I didn't give up my seat because I was tired, but that isn't true. I was not tired physically, or no more tired than I usually was at the end of a working day. I was not old, although some people have an image of me as being old then. I was forty-two. No the only tired I was, was tired of giving in.

Quoted in Herb Boyd, ed., *Autobiography of a People: Three Centuries of African American History Told by Those Who Lived It*. New York: Doubleday, 2000, pp. 369–70.

no other way to go except by bus. You can also afford to stay out of town for one day. If you work, take a cab, or walk. But please, children and grown-ups, don't ride the bus at all on Monday. Please stay off all buses Monday.[49]

At midnight, Robinson went to Alabama State College, where she was a professor. With the help of a colleague, she cut a mimeograph stencil and ran off thirty-five thousand handbills. The next morning, Robinson and two of her students loaded the handbills into her car and delivered them to all the black schools in the area. At each school, a WPC representative was on hand to ensure that the flyers were disseminated. During the remainder of

The Newspaper Report

■

The day following the Rosa Parks arrest, a small story about it was tucked on page 9A of the *Montgomery Advertiser*. Although some arrests were not mentioned at all, the simple account of the event is testimony that the writer—like the rest of the Montgomery community—had no inkling of what was to come. Like many later reports of the incident, this report communicates the inaccuracy that Parks was sitting in the white section of the bus; in fact, it was a seat at the front of the Negro section that she refused to relinquish.

Negro Jailed Here for "Overlooking" Bus Segregation

A Montgomery Negro woman was arrested by city police last night for ignoring a bus driver who directed her to sit in the rear of the bus.

The woman, Rosa Parks, 634 Cleveland Ave., was later released under $100 bond.

Bus operator J.F. Blake, 27 N. Lewis St., in notifying police, said a Negro woman sitting in the section reserved for whites refused to move to the Negro section.

When Officers F.B. Day and D.W. Mixon arrived where the bus was halted on Montgomery Street, they confirmed the driver's report.

Blake signed the warrant for her arrest under a section of the City Code that gives police powers to bus drivers in the enforcement of segregation aboard buses.

Montgomery Advertiser, "Negro Jailed Here for 'Overlooking' Bus Segregation," December 2, 1955, page 9A. http://nl.newsbank.com/nl-search/we/Archives?p_action=doc&p_docid=10D1602121B 0E0C0&p_docnum=2&p_theme=gannett&rs_site=montgomeryadvertiser&p_product=MGAB.

the day, WPC members dropped off bundles of leaflets at businesses and other places where blacks were likely to congregate.

The WPC's communication channels reached almost everyone in the African American community, but not all. Robinson recalls:

> Most of the people got the message, but there were outlying areas that didn't. One lone black woman, who was so faithful to her white lady, as she called it, went back to work and took one of the circulars to this woman so she would know what the blacks had planned. When the woman got it, she immediately called the media. After that, the television, the radio, the evening newspapers told those persons whom we had not reached that there would be a boycott.[50]

The Planning Meeting

Meanwhile, Nixon worked on garnering the support of other African American leaders and arranged for a meeting of Montgomery's ministers. Nixon later recalled the many calls he made early the morning after Parks's arrest:

> Number one, I called Ralph D. Abernathy. And he said he'd go along with it. Second, I called the late Reverend H. H. Hubbard. And I called Reverend [Martin Luther King Jr.], number three. Reverend King said, "Brother Nixon, let me think about it awhile and call me back." Well, I could see that. He's a new man in town, he don't know what it's all about. . . . So I went on and called eighteen other people, and I called him back and he said, "Yeah, Brother Nixon, I'll go along with it," and I said, "I'm glad of that, Reverend King, because I talked to eighteen other people; I told them to meet at your church at three o'clock."[51]

Roughly fifty people showed up at the Dexter Avenue Baptist Church that afternoon, including Abernathy, King, and Parks. (Nixon did not attend because he had to go to work.) There were long discussions about whether a boycott was the best approach. Parks describes the situation:

> Some of the ministers wanted to talk about how to support the protest, but others wanted to talk about whether or not to have a protest. Many of them left the meeting before any

Martin Luther King Jr. discusses plans for the bus boycott with advisers and organizers, including Rosa Parks (center).

decisions were made. But most of those who stayed agreed to talk about the protest in their Sunday sermons and to hold another meeting on Monday evening to decide if the protest should continue.[52]

The involvement of black churches proved to be a pivotal element in the success of the boycott. In Montgomery as throughout the South, the churches played a central role in the life of the African American community. Here, African Americans gathered with little or no interference from whites. Ministers used sermons to articulate a path of action and galvanize the community. Historian Peter B. Levy writes, "Among other things, the church served as a training ground for charismatic leaders, enlisted a mass and decentralized membership, accumulated a reservoir of money and fund-raising experiences, and reached a doctrine or ideology that at its core contradicted the ideology of white supremacy."[53]

"We Surprised Ourselves"

The planners of the boycott watched anxiously as Monday, December 5, the day of the boycott, dawned cold and overcast. They feared that rain would prompt people to ride the bus, but

Speech by Martin Luther King Jr.

At the mass meeting held on December 5, 1955, at the Holt Street Baptist Church, Martin Luther King Jr. outlined a course of action based on nonviolence, Christian love, and a dedication to justice.

We are not here advocating violence. We have overcome that. . . . Don't let anybody make us feel that we ought to be compared in our actions with the Ku Klux Klan or with the White Citizens' Councils. There will be no crosses burned at any bus stops in Montgomery. There will be no white persons pulled out of their homes and taken out to some distant road and murdered. There will be nobody among us who will stand up and defy the Constitution of this nation. . . .

We are not wrong in what we are doing. If we are wrong, then the Supreme Court of this Nation is wrong. If we are wrong, the Constitution of the United States is wrong. If we are wrong, God Almighty is wrong. . . . And we are determined here in Montgomery to work and fight until justice runs down like water and righteousness like a mighty stream.

We, the disinherited of this land, we who have been oppressed so long are tired of going through the long night of captivity. And we are reaching out for the daybreak of freedom and justice and equality. . . . Let us be Christian in all of our action. [But] it is not enough for us to talk about love. Love is one of the pinnacle parts of the Christian faith. There is another side called justice.

Quoted in Clayborne Carson, David J. Garrow, Gerald Gill, Vincent Harding, Darlene Clark Hine, eds., *The Eyes on the Prize Civil Rights Reader: Documents, Speeches, and Firsthand Accounts from the Black Freedom Struggle, 1954–1990*. New York: Penguin, 1991, pp. 49–50.

this cloud soon lifted as the first buses made their way down Montgomery's streets. Bus after bus rolled by without a single rider. Not only were there no black riders, there were also very few white passengers. "We surprised ourselves," Nixon later said. "Never before had black people demonstrated so clearly how much those city buses depended on their business. More important, never before had the black community of Montgomery united in protest against segregation on the buses."[54]

Trailing each bus were two white policemen on motorcycles. Robinson explains, "Rumors had spread that hundreds of black domestics had telephoned their 'white folks' that they would not be at work on Monday because they were 'afraid to ride the bus.'" The city responded by assigning the police escort to follow buses into predominantly black areas "to protect Negro riders" from "goon squads."[55]

The rumors proved unfounded. Perhaps whites wanted to believe that blacks did not ride the buses because they were too afraid, but in reality the boycott stemmed not from a fear of retaliation by their fellow blacks but rather because of the daily frustrations they experienced at the hands of bus drivers and the white establishment. Robinson points out that the police escort may have helped the boycott because the "few blacks who were going to ride were afraid that the police who were following the buses would hurt them."[56] The years of intimidation and abuse seemed to have backfired.

The leaders of the boycott had arranged for black taxicab drivers to provide rides to boycotters at the reduced fare of ten cents—the same price as taking the bus. African Americans also caught rides from friends who had cars. Others were picked up by whites whose primary interest was getting their domestic employees to their homes or other workers to their places of business. Thousands more walked to work and school.

Rosa Parks did not have time to watch the empty buses lumber up and down the city streets. She had to get to the courthouse for her trial. When she and Fred Gray pulled up to the courthouse, they found a crowd of about five hundred African Americans who had come to show their support and cheer on Parks. "Oh, she's so sweet," a high-pitched voice pierced the air. "They've messed with the wrong one now."[57]

Gray entered a plea of "not guilty" on Parks's behalf. After a trial that lasted less than half an hour, the judge found Parks guilty and fined her ten dollars, plus a four-dollar court fee.

The Montgomery Improvement Association Is Born

On Monday afternoon, the ministers and other leaders who had met on Friday came together again to decide whether to continue the boycott. Some argued that they had proven their point with the one-day boycott; others asked for their names to be left off any correspondence advocating the boycott's continuation. Nixon had little patience for the naysayers. "What you talking about?" he asked. "You guys have went around here and lived off these poor washerwomen all your lives and ain't never done nothing for 'em. And now you got a chance to do something for 'em, you talkin' about you don't want the white folks to know it."[58] He told the others to stop acting like "little boys." "Now's the time to be mens," Nixon concluded.[59]

King was the first to respond. "Brother Nixon, I'm not a coward," he said. "I don't want anybody to be a coward."[60]

The group agreed to let the community decide whether to continue the boycott. Following the example in Baton Rouge two years earlier, a mass meeting was scheduled for seven o'clock that evening. In preparation, the group of ministers gave themselves a name—the Montgomery Improvement Association (MIA)—and elected Martin Luther King as chair. King

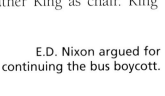

E.D. Nixon argued for continuing the bus boycott.

was just twenty-six years old. He had recently completed his doctoral coursework at Boston University, and the Dexter Avenue Baptist Church was his first assignment as a minister. The others thought King's recent arrival in Montgomery would be an asset to the group because King had not had time to make enemies in either the black or the white community. A few of his colleagues also had heard him speak and were impressed by his oratorical abilities.

The First Community Meeting

People began to congregate in the mid-afternoon for the seven o'clock meeting, and by five o'clock every seat was taken. Subsequent arrivals spilled out onto the grounds and sidewalks nearby. Martin Luther King Jr. described the scene:

> Within five blocks of the church I noticed a traffic jam. Cars were lined up as far as I could see on both sides of the street. . . . I had to park at least four blocks from the church, and as I started walking I noticed that hundreds of people were standing outside. In the dark night, police cars circled slowly around the area, surveying the orderly, patient, and good-humored crowd.[61]

The organizers set up a loudspeaker system so that the crowd outside—estimated at three to four thousand people—could hear what was going on. Nixon spoke first:

> You who are afraid, you better get your hat and coat and go home. This is going to be a long drawn-out affair. For years and years I've been talking about how I didn't want the children

Martin Luther King Jr. was elected chair of the Montgomery Improvement Association.

who came along behind me to have to suffer the indignities that I've suffered all these years. Well, I've changed my mind—I want to enjoy some of that freedom myself.[62]

Nixon's comments were followed by speeches by several ministers. These speeches were broken up by prayers and hymns. "The passion that fired the meeting was seen as the thousands of voices joined in singing," wrote Joe Azbell, the city editor of Montgomery's daily newspaper who was just one of five whites at the meeting. "The voices thundered through the church."[63]

The Principles of Nonviolent Resistance

Martin Luther King Jr. proved to be particularly eloquent. King spoke of the injustice of segregation. He spoke of protest. He argued that regardless of how angry the members of the audience were, they should not respond with violence. King based his principles on the teachings and experiences of Mohandas Gandhi in India. Years earlier, Gandhi had used nonviolent resistance to win independence for his fellow Indians from the British. India's experience showed that, by massive civil disobedience and non-cooperation, people could win their rights without violence or bloodshed. King believed this was in keeping with Christian principles. "The only weapon that we have in our hands this evening is the weapon of protest," he told the boycotters. "There will be no white persons pulled out of their homes and taken out on some distant road and murdered. There will be nobody among us who will stand up and defy the Constitution. . . . We are going to have a real protest. We are going to keep walking."[64]

When the question about whether to end the boycott was raised, the crowd answered with a resounding, unanimous "No!"

The boycott clearly had found an audience. In *They Walked to Freedom*, Kenneth M. Hare writes, "The arrest of Rosa Parks was a small breach in a dam of pent-up frustration and anger among the black citizens of Montgomery. The leak that started with her arrest on December 1 had become a torrent by December 5, when the Montgomery Improvement Association was born and the Montgomery Bus Boycott became a reality."[65]

The meeting showed the new MIA leaders that the African American community was fully behind the boycott. They confirmed their willingness to fight for justice—even if it was "a long

King Reflects on the First Boycott Meeting

—■—

In a 1956 address at the first annual meeting of the Institute for Nonviolence and Social Change, Martin Luther King looked back on the events of December 5, 1955.

The deliberations of that brisk and cold night in December will long be stenciled on the mental sheets of succeeding generations. Little did we know on that night that we were starting a movement that would rise to international proportions; a movement whose lofty echoes would ring in the ears of people of every nation; a movement that would stagger and astound the imagination of the oppressor, while leaving a glittering star of hope etched in the midnight skies of the oppressed. Little did we know that night that we were starting a movement that would gain the admiration of men of goodwill all over the world. But God still has a mysterious way to perform His wonders. It seems that God decided to use Montgomery as the proving ground for the struggle and triumph of freedom and justice in America. It is one of the ironies of our day that Montgomery, the Cradle of the Confederacy, is being transformed into Montgomery, the cradle of freedom and justice.

Quoted in The Papers of Martin Luther King Jr., "Facing the Challenge of a New Day." www.stanford.edu/group/King/publications/papers/vol3/561203.000-Facing_the_Challenge_of_a_New_Age,_annual_address_at_the_first_annual_Institute_on_Nonviolence_and_Social_Change.htm.

drawn-out affair."[66] Joe Azbell later wrote that "the meeting was much like an old-fashioned revival with loud applause added. It proved beyond any doubt that there was a discipline among Negroes that many whites had doubted. It was almost a military discipline combined with emotion."[67]

A few days prior, the leaders of the boycott had hoped that more than half of the African Americans who rode Montgomery's buses would heed the plea to stay off the buses for one day. Some leaders thought that a one-day boycott was all they could ask of their African American brethren. The exuberance of their followers far exceeded their expectations. "A miracle had taken place," King said later. "The once dormant and quiescent Negro community was now fully awake."[68]

The historic Montgomery bus boycott had begun.

Chapter Four

The Boycott Continues

When the boycott of Montgomery's buses began, no one expected it to last very long. Most boycotts lasted a day; a few went for a couple of weeks. None lasted as long as the boycott in Montgomery, where African Americans found rides, took taxis, and walked to avoid the bus for over a year.

Many people assume that the aim of the Montgomery bus boycott was the desegregation of the city's buses. Admittedly, most African Americans probably would have liked to eliminate segregation on the buses, but the leaders of the boycott recognized the peril of demanding integration. Jo Ann Robinson explains, "To admit that black Americans were seeking to integrate would have been too much; there probably would have been much bloodshed and arrests of those who dared to disclose such an idea!"[69]

Robinson later elaborated on this topic when she wrote, "For the sake of a peaceful fight, we kept silent on integration. . . . We were not obnoxious about it, but quietly demanded it."[70]

The boycott's leaders identified three demands that the city and bus company would have to meet for them to end the boycott:

Gandhi and Nonviolence

Martin Luther King Jr. applied many of the techniques of non-violent resistance that Mohandas Gandhi had used success-fully in India. In her award-winning book about the U.S. civil rights movement, Diane McWhorter describes Gandhi's influence:

> The long campaign to free India from British colonial rule was led by Mohandas K. Gandhi, an English-trained lawyer who urged his native country's lowliest "untouchables" not to "submit to injustice from anyone." His strategy was known as *satyagraha*, which meant "truth" (*satya* in Sanskrit) backed by "firmness" or "persistence" (*agraha*). Gandhi's most famous nonviolent protest was the Salt March of 1930, in which he and his followers illegally took salt from seawater. By British law in India, only the government could produce salt; so poor people were forced to buy something available free in nature.
>
> Gandhi and his followers went to jail for breaking unjust laws. This strategy of nonviolence did not mean being soft or weak. It meant peacefully but forcefully resisting an evil system. And it was not for cowards: In 1948, Gandhi was assassinated by a religious fanatic.

Diane McWhorter, *A Dream of Freedom: The Civil Rights Movement from 1954 to 1968.* New York: Scholastic, 2004, p. 43.

Martin Luther King Jr. based his principles of nonviolence on the teachings of Mohandas Gandhi (pictured).

courtesy from bus drivers, a system in which blacks could sit from the rear toward the front and whites from the front toward the rear until all seats were taken, and the hiring of black bus drivers for predominantly black routes.

Despite the seemingly benign nature of such demands, the city refused to give ground. Ken Hare writes:

> It is ironic that in the early days of the boycott, when MIA officials were still negotiating with officials of the city and the bus line, their demands stopped far short of ending segregation on city buses. If city officials had given in to these modest demands, they would have derailed the boycott and quite likely have caused the focus of the Civil Rights Movement to have shifted to some city other than Montgomery.[71]

Getting Around

Winning even minor concessions would require sacrifice, however. Thousands of African Americans had relied on the buses to get to and from work and school every day. Thousands more used the buses to go shopping or to visit friends and family across town. For over a year, these people had to find other ways to get where they needed to be.

Many boycotters walked everywhere. Each morning, tides of black people flowed down Montgomery's sidewalks as empty buses passed by. Others rode bicycles or even mules or horse-drawn buggies.

The white community took measures to shut down the boycott almost immediately. Just a few days after the boycott began, bus officials asked the city commission for permission to close routes to black communities. They argued that they would lose money if they continued to service those areas. As a result, the people in black neighborhoods could not ride the buses even if they wanted to. The city also began to enforce a previously ignored city ordinance that set the minimum taxi fare at forty-five cents and threatened to arrest black taxi drivers who offered rides for less than this.

Within a few days, the Montgomery Improvement Association began organizing carpools to get people where they needed to be. African Americans who owned cars volunteered their use, sometimes driving the cars themselves to get people where they needed to go. By December 13, 1955, roughly three hundred people had volunteered the use of their cars. The MIA used a downtown parking lot as a transfer station, bringing people to and from various parts of the city.

This ad hoc carpool system soon developed into an efficient, cost-effective means of transportation. The MIA's new transportation system included regular routes and pickup and delivery points. Fueled by donations, the churches bought cars for use in the transportation system. MIA volunteers served as dispatchers and drivers. The MIA system provided transportation from 5:30 A.M. until 12:30 at night. An estimated thirty thousand people relied on the system daily to get to and from work.

Leadership and Communication

The MIA held monthly meetings open to the African American community. During these meetings, hundreds of African Americans joined together to pray, hear from the MIA leaders, voice their concerns, and recommit to the cause. Jo Ann Robinson also produced a newsletter to keep the community informed about new developments in the boycott and strategies for getting people from one place to another. In addition to providing practical information to Montgomery's African Americans, the newsletter helped to get word out beyond the community. Robinson wrote:

> The plight of the Montgomery people was explained monthly in these pages and the national and even worldwide response was amazing. In a very short time, money was being mailed to MIA in large quantities. Any newsletter brought in thousands of dollars. The news items brought more. Thousands of dollars began to flow into MIA's treasury and did not cease for 13 months.[72]

Across the nation, black churches raised money to support the boycott and collected donations of clothing and shoes. "Many people needed those things because they were out of work and unable to buy clothing," explained Rosa Parks later. "Those who had jobs wore out many pairs of shoes walking to and from work."[73]

Early Effects of the Boycott

The boycott proved effective from the beginning. On January 5, 1956, just a month after the boycott had started, so few people were riding city buses that the bus company's expenses—gas and salaries for drivers—far exceeded its income. The superintendent of the bus company estimated that it was losing at least four hundred dollars a day, but he was grossly underestimating his losses. Donnie Williams writes, "In truth, the company was losing much more."[74]

Mayor W.A. "Tacky" Gayle was vehement in his opposition to the boycott and reluctant to negotiate, even as the bus company and business interests urged the city to find a compromise. "We are going to hold our stand," Gayle declared. "We are not going to be a part of any program that will get Negroes to ride the buses again at the price of the destruction of our heritage and way of life."[75]

The bus company had a contract with the city to provide service, so ceasing operations was not an option. Mayor Gayle asked white people to ride the buses more frequently, but most ignored the request. Some white residents said that they were afraid to take the bus because of reports of violence. Others were used to driving and saw no reason to change. The city agreed to allow the company to increase fares, but to no avail. Each day, the bus company continued to lose money.

Speaking on behalf of the city commission, Mayor Gayle urged whites not to help the boycotters. "When a white person gives a Negro a single penny for transportation or helps a Negro with his transportation, even if it's a block ride he is helping the Negro radicals who lead the boycott," the mayor said. "The Negroes have made their own bed and the whites should let them sleep in it."[76]

Gayle was especially critical of the white housewives who drove their maids, nannies, and other domestic helpers to and from work. He demanded that the white women of Montgomery stop giving their help rides and said that anyone who would not take the bus should be fired. Virginia Durr later recalled that Montgomery's white women "were just furious" at the mayor. "Okay," they said, "if Tacky Gayle wants to come out here and do my washing and ironing and cleaning and cooking and look after my children, he can do it, but unless he does, I'm going to get Mary or Sally or Suzy."[77]

White women justified their actions by claiming that they and their help had nothing to do with the boycott, and offered excuses for providing rides. They might claim that the bus had broken down, for instance, or say that their maid was too scared to ride the bus.

A usually crowded Montgomery, Alabama, bus has only two riders during the boycott.

Blacks also denied that they were participating in the boycott. In response to questions about why they were walking, they might reply simply that they were enjoying the nice weather or that they were just going a couple of blocks. They would say that they accepted a ride from a friend or relative who just happened to be going in their direction. Virginia Durr explains the system of complicity that arose: "The black women needed those jobs. They weren't paid very much, but that's all the income many of them had. They couldn't afford to say, 'I'm supporting the boycott.' So the white women lied and the black women lied. And the maids kept coming and the white women kept driving them back and forth to work."[78]

The City Gets Tough

In January, as the boycott showed no signs of slowing, the city announced a "get tough" policy. African Americans waiting for rides were cited for loitering. Carpool drivers were arrested for overloading their vehicles. The MIA warned drivers to avoid speeding and to obey all traffic laws, but the police continued to find fault. Robinson remembers:

> Every black person would get a traffic ticket two and three times a week. One time, I stopped at the corner right above

the college where I lived, and a policeman drove up and said, "Well, you stayed there too long that time." And the next day or two I'd come up, "Well, you didn't stay quite long enough this time." There was no need of arguing, we just took them. We just paid them.[79]

As the boycott wore on, downtown merchants began to feel the effects. By February 1, 1956, businesses downtown claimed losses of over 1 million dollars. In February, the bus company capitulated—management said that it would no longer enforce Jim Crow laws.

City officials were not going to let this happen, however. They countered with a threat to arrest bus drivers who did not enforce the laws. A court ordered that the company could not legally desegregate its buses. A few weeks later, the city used an outdated law to claim that the actions of the boycotters were illegal. Eighty-nine of the boycott leaders were arrested, including Martin Luther King Jr., Ralph Abernathy, and Rosa Parks.

The arrests of Montgomery's boycotters captured the attention of the nation. Throughout the country, front-page stories of the arrests showed photos of King, Parks, and other boycotters being fingerprinted. Money and donations—as well as reporters and supporters—streamed into Montgomery.

King was among the first to be tried. During the March 19 trial, witnesses came forth to testify on King's behalf. "People were not reluctant to speak out,"[80] Parks recalls. For the first time, African Americans were not scared to tell their stories of abuse at the hands of bus drivers and police officers.

A police officer gives a parking ticket to an African American man during the Montgomery bus boycott.

Why Direct Action?

Martin Luther King Jr. was arrested numerous times for his role in the civil rights movement. In the following letter, which he wrote to his "dear fellow clergymen" while in a Birmingham jail, Martin Luther King set out to clarify the meaning of nonviolent resistance.

You may well ask: "Why direct action? Why sit-ins, marches, and so forth? Isn't negotiation a better path?" You are quite right in calling for negotiation. Indeed, this is the very purpose of direct action. Nonviolent direct action seeks to create such a crisis and foster such a tension that a community which has constantly refused to negotiate is forced to confront the issue. It seeks to dramatize the issue so that it can no longer be ignored. My citing the creation of tension as part of the work of the nonviolent resister may sound rather shocking. But I must confess that I am not afraid of the word "tension." I have earnestly opposed violent tension, but there is a type of constructive, nonviolent tension which is necessary for growth. Just as Socrates felt that it was necessary to create a tension in the mind so that individuals could rise from the bondage of myths and half-truths to the unfettered realm of creative analysis and objective appraisal, so must we see the need for nonviolent gadflies to create the kinds of tension in society that will help men rise from the dark depths of prejudice and racism to the majestic heights of understanding and brotherhood.

Martin Luther King Jr., "Letter from Birmingham Jail." www.stanford.edu/group/King/popular_requests/frequentdocs/birmingham.pdf.

The judge was not persuaded, however. He found King guilty and ordered him to pay a $500 fine or serve over a year in jail. In reflecting on his arrest, King said, "I was proud of my crime. It was the crime of joining my people in a nonviolent protest against injustice."[81]

Intimidation and Violence

As official tactics failed, whites turned to intimidation. The membership of the White Citizens' Council (WCC) doubled during the course of the boycott. The members of the WCC had taken a pledge to "help defeat the NAACP, integration, mongrelism, socialism, Communist ideologies, and one-world government, and to help preserve the U.S. Constitution and the bill of rights, states' rights, segregation, and our God-fearing American nation."[82]

The WCC was formed as a political entity, but like the Ku Klux Klan (KKK), its members sometimes resorted to violence. Groups of whites roughed up African Americans as they waited for their rides, and these groups threatened violence to others. One member of the KKK wrote later: "We didn't care what the city was going to do with them [blacks and the black leaders]; we knew they were doing what they wanted to do: they were not riding the buses and they were standing up in City Hall and talking like they owned the place. We knew damn well we had to do something. This whole thing was getting out of hand."[83]

Vandals slashed tires or put sugar or sand in the gas tanks of black-owned vehicles so that they could not be driven. The boycott's leaders received threatening phone calls and letters. By the middle of January, King was receiving as many as forty letters a day. Many, signed "KKK" (for the Ku Klux Klan), simply said, "Get out of town or else."[84] Others presented "half-truths" arguing that segregation was called for in the Bible. Still others were filled with words of hatred and abuse.

These were not idle threats. On January 30, 1956, a bomb exploded on the Kings's porch. King was not at home, but his wife, Coretta, and their baby girl narrowly escaped injury. "When King's house was bombed, it affected the whole black community," Rufus Lewis later said. "The damage wasn't bad, but it was intended to intimidate. It did just the opposite of intimidating. It roused the Negroes in the community to stand up, not to run and hide. They lost in their effort to intimidate. They only gave more courage to King's family and the blacks in the community to stand up with him."[85]

Angry blacks congregated at King's home. Some arrived fully armed, prepared to take on the white perpetrators. As King stood

Martin Luther King Jr. (second from right) stands on his porch after it was bombed and urges a continued commitment to nonviolence.

on his damaged porch, he reminded the crowd of the movement's commitment to nonviolence: "He who lives by the sword will perish by the sword. . . . We must love our white brothers no matter what they do to us. We must meet hate with love. What we are doing is just, and God is with us."[86]

Joe Azbell had raced to King's house to cover the bombing for the *Montgomery Advertiser* and had arrived in time to hear King calm the crowd. "That night King made a believer out of me," Azbell recalls. "He stood there and quieted that angry mob. I know that if he had not spoken as he had, violence would have erupted."[87]

But not everyone became a believer. Just two days later, a bomb was thrown onto the porch of E.D. Nixon's home. Again, no one was hurt, but Nixon tried to convince his wife, Arlet, to

A Reminder of White Support

Even before the bus boycott, Martin Luther King Jr. reminded his followers to remain calm in the face of violence, as in this 1955 sermon delivered at the Dexter Avenue Baptist Church.

> The Negro who experiences bitter and agonizing circumstances as a result of some ungodly white person is tempted to look upon all white persons as evil, if he fails to look beyond his circumstances. But the minute he looks beyond his circumstances and sees the whole of the situation, he discovers that some of the most implacable and vehement advocates of racial equality are consecrated white persons. We must never forget that such a noble organization as the National Association for the Advancement of Colored People was organized by whites, and even to this day gains a great deal of support from Northern and Southern white persons.

Quoted in Clarence Clayborne, ed., *The Autobiography of Martin Luther King, Jr.*, The Martin Luther King, Jr., Research and Education Institute. www.stanford.edu/group/King//publications/.

leave town until the threat of violence had subsided. She refused. "They're trying to make you quit, but don't do it," she said. "I'd rather be the widow of a man who had the courage to fight than the wife of a coward."[88]

Jo Ann Robinson was also targeted. Gangs of whites threw bricks through her front window, and police officers poured acid on her new car. "At first I thought it was a terrible tragedy," Robinson recalled as she looked at the holes in her car. "I cried, and then I said, 'Well, you know, these are beautiful spots.'"[89]

White Support

Whites who helped the black boycotters also became targets of violence. Simply offering a ride to a black pedestrian could be dangerous. But a few whites persisted. "Now and then, out of nowhere, a white driver would pick up a Negro walking down the street," recalled Nixon. "But that didn't happen often."[90]

Sarah Herbert was among the whites who continued to drive her maid and other blacks where they needed to go. Her husband, Woodson Draught, an FBI agent, risked his life to attend KKK meetings to gain information about what they were doing and to take down the license plate numbers of Klan members. "My husband was very enthusiastic about [gaining civil rights for blacks]," Herbert recalled, "but at the time, he couldn't work openly, so he did it behind the scenes."[91]

In addition to offering rides to black boycotters, some whites actively boycotted the bus themselves. Nixon tells of a story in which he offered a ride to a white man who was walking in the pouring rain. When the man got in the car, he said, "I promised myself I wouldn't ride the bus again 'til all of your demands have been met. And I don't own a car."[92] Nixon gave him a card with the phone number of the MIA pickup station and suggested that the man call next time he needed a ride. He called a few days later explaining that he had "a bunch of groceries and needed assistance."[93] A member of the MIA carpool picked him up.

Robert Graetz, a white minister of an all-black church, was one of the most ardent supporters of the boycott. From the beginning, he urged his parishioners to support the boycott. He was the only white member of the MIA and helped to organize the carpool system. He also served as a driver every morning. Graetz

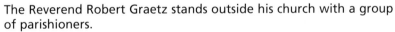

The Reverend Robert Graetz stands outside his church with a group of parishioners.

also succeeded in inspiring others. At one point, a woman identifying herself as "an old white lady" and a member of "an old family who knows all the city officials"[94] called Graetz to offer her Oldsmobile for the carpool.

Graetz paid dearly for his commitment to the cause. He and his family were ostracized by the white community. Threatening letters flooded his mailbox, and his tires were slashed. His house was bombed twice during the boycott and once immediately after it ended.

The violence only strengthened the resolve of those committed to the boycott. "Dr. King used to talk about the reality that some of us were going to die and that if any of us were afraid to die we really shouldn't be there,"[95] Graetz later said.

The Legal Fight

In conjunction with the boycott, black leaders attempted to use the legal system to put an end to discrimination on the buses. Gray later wrote that he felt a lawsuit was crucial to bolstering the commitment of those who were conducting the boycott, giving them hope that they could prevail even if city officials stood firm in the face of the boycott itself. "We concluded that if we were ever going to get anywhere, we would have to go to the federal court,"[96] Gray said.

On February 1, 1956, attorneys Fred Gray and Charles Langford filed a lawsuit on behalf of four female plaintiffs, all of whom had been treated unfairly on city buses because of their race. The case became known as *Browder v. Gayle*. (The plaintiffs in the case were Aurelia Browder, a homemaker; Susie McDonald, a black woman in her seventies; Claudette Colvin, the fifteen-year-old who had been arrested several months previously for refusing to give up her bus seat; and Mary Louise Smith, an eighteen-year-old who had been arrested in October 1955.)

In the suit, the lawyers no longer sought a simple change in the bus company's practice of requiring African Americans to give up their seats for white riders, but instead sought to end segregation altogether. "We didn't ask the federal court for [the original] point we [had] approached the city with," Gray explained. "We filed to end segregation."[97] The attorneys for the plaintiffs argued that the 1954 Supreme Court ruling in *Brown v. Board of Educa-*

tion of Topeka, Kansas applied not only to education, but to public transportation as well.

The City Appeals

On June 4, 1956, the special panel of three federal judges ruled in favor of the black plaintiffs. In a two-to-one vote, the judges declared that Alabama's state and local laws requiring segregation on buses violated the Fourteenth Amendment of the U.S. Constitution, which guarantees equal protection. Attorneys for the city of Montgomery and the state of Alabama immediately filed an appeal.

Attorney Fred Gray argues a court case filed on behalf of four black women who were treated unfairly on Montgomery city buses.

The African American community responded by voting to continue the bus boycott until all appeals had been exhausted, even though they realized this could take months.

Meanwhile, city leaders continued their attempts to end the boycott. City officials convinced local insurance companies to refuse to insure the vehicles used in the carpools. Each time the MIA purchased insurance from a new company, the policy would suddenly be canceled. This happened at least four times before King resolved the problem by obtaining insurance from Lloyds of London, a British insurance company, through an Atlanta agent.

In June, the NAACP was banned from operating in Alabama after the attorney general argued that its actions had "resulted in violations of our laws and . . . in many instances [had created] a breach of the peace."[98] The judge's order stated emphatically that the NAACP was "organizing, supporting, and financing an illegal boycott by Negro residents of Montgomery."[99]

Black leaders in Montgomery responded by forming a new organization, called the Alabama Christian Movement for Human Rights. The group adopted a resolution pledged to remove from society "any forms of second-class citizenship" and to do away with segregation. At its first meeting in Birmingham, the leader of the new organization praised the bus boycotters in Montgomery "for conducting themselves in the struggle so valiantly, and without rancor, hate and smear, and above all, without violence."[100]

Chapter Five

Victory

Montgomery's white leaders continued to seek ways to put an end to the boycott. In late October, lawyers for the city cited a provision of the Code of Alabama stating that "any firm, association, or corporation using the streets of any city for the construction or operation of any public utility cannot do so without first obtaining permission of the city commission"[101] and declared that, since the city had granted the MIA no such permission, it was operating illegally. The hearing was set for November 13.

King assured the community that the carpool would continue to operate. "In the face of a threatening injunction," King said, "the Negro community is determined to struggle and sacrifice until the walls of injustice are finally crushed by the battering rams of surging justice. We are simply offering free rides to the Negro citizenry of Montgomery through the services of our church."[102]

"A Glorious Daybreak"

The morning of November 13, the boycott's leaders and city officials went to the courthouse to hear the judge's decision about the carpool. King and the other leaders of the MIA watched as

---

The Bulletin

■

As the leaders of the boycott waited for news about whether the Montgomery Improvement Association's carpool would be shut down, a reporter handed Martin Luther King Jr. a bulletin that read:

> WASHINGTON (AP)—The Supreme Court today upheld a decision holding unconstitutional Alabama and Montgomery, Ala., laws requiring racial segregation on buses.
>
> The decision by a special three-judge U.S. District Court in Montgomery was appealed by the city's board of commissioners and by the Alabama Public Service Commission. Each filed separately.
>
> Today's Supreme Court action was unanimous.

Quoted in Donnie Williams and Wayne Greenhaw, *The Thunder of Angels: The Montgomery Bus Boycott and the People Who Broke the Back of Jim Crow.* Chicago: Lawrence Hill, 2006, p. 239.

---

the mayor and police commissioners were called into a back room, followed by the city's attorneys. Reporters bustled about. Finally, a reporter handed King a bulletin that stated: "The Supreme Court today upheld a decision holding unconstitutional Alabama and Montgomery, Ala., laws requiring racial segregation on buses. . . . Today's Supreme Court action was unanimous." [103]

Montgomery's black leaders hailed the decision. King called it "a glorious daybreak to end a long night of enforced segregation."[104]

That night, the boycotters held two mass meetings at black churches on opposite ends of the town. Thousands of men, women, and children crammed into the churches and spilled out onto the sidewalks and into the street. King made an appearance at each of the meetings.

King and others spoke of what the ruling meant. Yes, it meant the end to segregation on the city's buses, but the ruling would not take effect until the paperwork was completed. The city had vowed to continue to enforce bus segregation laws until then.

The next day, the judge ruled that the MIA's carpool was illegal. Since anyone caught driving or riding in the church-owned vehicles would likely be arrested, the MIA suspended the carpool's operations. But King announced that the boycott would continue. "For these three or four days," King announced, "we will continue to walk and share rides with friends."[105]

The Long Walk to Freedom

King was optimistic in his assessment of how long it would take for the Supreme Court's ruling to become official. It took over a month for the paperwork to reach Montgomery. In the meantime, African Americans did what they had always done. They improvised. The people of Montgomery walked through the cold of winter and through the heat of summer. "When we heard the words that the Court ruled in our favor, we were happy. Everybody cheered," recalls Nixon. "But the people felt heavy-hearted and dog-tired. They lifted their feet when they were going to work in the morning, but they dragged them along the ground when they came home at night."[106]

African Americans walk to work during the Montgomery bus boycott.

Gussie Nesbitt, a participant in the boycott, remembers her resolve to continue until the boycott had achieved its aims: "I walked because I wanted everything to be better for us. . . . I wanted to be one of them that tried to make it better. I didn't want somebody else to make it better for me. I walked. I never attempted to take the bus. Never. I was tired, but I didn't have no desire to get on the bus."[107]

Children also boycotted the buses. Seven-year-old Bernice Robinson and her two sisters walked over eight miles a day twice a week to take piano lessons. "We walked because it was right and because it was wrong to get on the bus," Bernice remembered. "And it wasn't easy, either . . . because sometimes white folks would go by and blow the horn or yell things at us."[108]

A Vow to Fight for Segregation

Following the ruling, white leaders in Montgomery warned that attempts to integrate the buses would likely result in violence. The head of Montgomery's White Citizens' Council predicted that "any attempt to enforce this decision will inevitably lead to riot and bloodshed."[109]

City and state officials also announced that they did not accept integration as inevitable. Mayor Gayle stated that the city would "do all legal things necessary to continue enforcement of our segregation laws and ordinances of all kinds . . . to protect the peoples of both races, and to promote order in our city."[110] One state representative said that he had "25 or 30 segregation bills in process of drafting."[111] Another said that the state legislature might "authorize" bus drivers to tell people where to sit "for the convenience of the passengers."[112]

Preparing the Community

Meanwhile, the boycott's leaders prepared the black community for returning to the buses. They anticipated resistance to the change and wanted to avoid violence wherever possible. "In mass meeting after mass meeting we stressed nonviolence," King recalled. "The prevailing theme was that 'we must not take this as a victory over the white man, but as a victory for justice and democracy.'"[113]

The MIA leaders urged blacks not to respond to insults or taunts. Violence was to be met as it always had—with nonviolent

African Americans take part in an exercise to learn how to demonstrate goodwill to whites on newly integrated buses.

resistance. Blacks were not to back down—they had fought too hard to ride the buses as equal Americans—but they should avoid confrontations. The MIA's training programs included role playing. Chairs were lined up in rows at the front of the church to mimic the bus. A participant was chosen to play the part of the bus driver, and others played the role of black and white passengers. The black passengers were shown how to respond to insults or even physical abuse from hostile whites. The MIA facilitated a general discussion at the end of each session to reiterate the importance of avoiding violence and to share suggestions for handling different types of confrontations. "You must keep smiling," King explained. "When you step aboard the bus, smile. Put a smile in your heart. Let it glow from within. That is the only way you will be able to manage the hurt."[114]

MIA leaders also went to high schools and colleges to talk to students about how to deal with whites when they resumed taking the bus. Ministers used the pulpit to reiterate the importance of showing love to one's enemy and conducted sessions on anger management and demonstrated nonviolent resistance in action.

The MIA also distributed a list of "Suggestions for Integrating the Buses." This leaflet reminded passengers to "observe ordinary rules of courtesy and good behavior" and suggested that blacks should be "quiet but friendly; proud, but not arrogant; joyous, but not boisterous." The boycott also asked blacks not to boast or brag. The recommendations reiterated the principles of nonviolence: "If cursed, do not curse back. If pushed, do not push back. If struck, do not strike back, but evidence love and goodwill at all times."[115]

The white community made no similar appeals, however. King later wrote, "We tried to get the white ministerial alliance to make a simple statement calling for courtesy and Christian brotherhood, but in spite of the favorable response of a few ministers, Robert Graetz reported that the majority 'dared not get involved in such a controversial issue.'"[116] Although King wrote that he was deeply disappointed by the lack of white involvement, he was hardly surprised. It was still dangerous for whites to take a public stand against segregation.

The Return to the Bus

On December 20, 1956, the Supreme Court's decision took effect. Throughout Montgomery—and beyond—African Ameri-

Rosa Parks on Racism Today

———————————————■———————————————

In a 1999 memoir, Rosa Parks reminds us that although laws have outlawed segregation, America still has a ways to go in wiping out prejudice and racism.

All those laws against segregation have been passed, and all that progress has been made. But a whole lot of white people's hearts have not been changed. Dr. King used to talk about the fact that if a law was changed, it might not change hearts but it would offer some protection. He was right. We now have some protection, but there is still much racism and racial violence. . . .

Sometimes I do feel pretty sad about some of the events that have taken place recently. I try to keep hope alive anyway, but that's not always the easiest thing to do. I have spent over half my life teaching love and brotherhood, and I feel that it is better to continue to try to teach or live equality and love than it would be to have hatred or prejudice. Everyone living together in peace and harmony and love . . . that's the goal that we seek, and I think that the more people there are who reach that state of mind, the better we will all be.

Rosa Parks and Jim Haskins, *Rosa Parks: My Story.* New York: Puffin, 1999, pp. 187–88.

cans were jubilant. Georgia Gilmore recalls listening to gospel music when a news report interrupted to announce that the Supreme Court's ruling had become final: "We were so happy. We felt that we had accomplished something that no one ever thought would happen in the city of Montgomery. Being able to ride the bus and sit anyplace . . . was something that hadn't happened before. . . . In the beginning you thought, well, maybe it wouldn't last. But still you would give it a try. And we did."[117]

Another community meeting was scheduled for the evening of December 20. "We just rejoiced together," recalled Jo Ann Robinson.

"We had won self-respect. We had won a feeling that we had achieved, had accomplished. We felt that we were somebody, that somebody had to listen to us, that we had forced the white man to give what we knew was part of our own citizenship."[118] The blacks jubilantly voted to end the boycott.

The next day, blacks in Montgomery returned to the city buses. At 5:55 A.M., E.D. Nixon, Martin Luther King Jr., Ralph Abernathy, and Glenn Smiley, a white civil rights activist from New York who had come to Montgomery as an observer, stood at a bus stop surrounded by reporters and photographers from across the country. When the bus pulled up to the stop, they stepped aboard and took seats in the front of the bus.

"We just rode," Nixon remembers. "It was the best ride I ever had in my life, just riding through downtown and out to the west and back again, going nowhere but feeling like we was heading to heaven."[119]

After 381 days, blacks could finally rest their feet and ride the bus to wherever they wanted to go.

Leaders of the Montgomery bus boycott stand at a bus stop following the Supreme Court ruling that city and state laws requiring segregated buses were illegal.

The Tough Transition

No change of this magnitude is ever easy. The leaders of the African American community knew that the fight was not over. King used the pulpit to warn his congregation that a legal victory was but one step toward freedom: "Just because we have won in court, life will not suddenly become easy. The travails will not vanish. The hills will not suddenly flatten. The valleys will not suddenly rise. The road you travel will not be paved with gold. Not yet! Heaven does not exist on this earth. If it did, there would be no promised land."[120]

The first day went relatively smoothly. Several blacks reported that white men and women had called them names or pushed them roughly. An elderly man slapped a black woman who refused to move from her seat in the front of the bus. But the black riders remembered King's teachings and did not retaliate.

Within a few days, however, the uneasy calm was punctuated by a string of violent episodes. On December 23, a shotgun blast was fired into King's home. The next evening—Christmas Eve—five white men jumped out of a car, beat a fifteen-year-old black girl as she stepped off the bus, jumped back into the car, and roared off. Snipers began firing on the newly integrated buses. On December 26, two buses were shot at by hidden gunmen. Two days later, someone fired at a bus twice in the same evening, hitting a young black woman in both legs. By December 29, five buses had been fired upon.

As with many other crimes in which whites took out their anger on black victims, the city did little to catch the perpetrators. City officials made a public announcement in which they said they would take no special measures to prevent violence. Instead, bus service was suspended after five o'clock. This meant that anyone working a typical nine-to-five shift could not get home from work by bus.

The violence soon spread beyond the buses and into Montgomery's neighborhoods. On Thursday, January 10, a gang of whites bombed four black churches and the homes of Ralph Abernathy and Robert Graetz. Two days later, a black taxi company and another home were bombed. Twelve sticks of dynamite also were found smoldering on the porch of the Kings' home, but they were snuffed out before they could do any damage.

Montgomery's citizens began to fear for their safety. "The issue now has passed beyond segregation," read an editorial in the *Montgomery Advertiser*. "The issue now *is whether it is safe to live in Montgomery*." The editorial further incited the city to take action by claiming that the violence was "blackening this city's name. . . . Those who are at this moment seeking enactment of unbearable civil rights legislation welcome such events, for they serve their cause."[121]

The city could no longer ignore the violence. On January 30, police arrested seven white men and charged them with the bombings and shooting attacks. Although two of the men confessed to throwing the bombs, the all-white jury found them not guilty and the judge set them free.

Gradually, the violence in Montgomery ceased. Blacks and whites boarded the buses, paid their fares, and rode without incident. Donnie Williams writes:

> In the days that followed the first wave of violent reaction to the Supreme Court's ruling, little by little, hardly noticed by midsummer of 1957, more and more blacks stepped aboard the buses, paid their fares, and sat in the front seats. Fewer and fewer whites rode the buses, but those who did sat quietly near the majority of black riders. There were few incidents of violence.[122]

The Civil Rights Movement Takes Wing

When asked what the boycott meant to the world, Robert Graetz quips, "Do I have an hour?" Graetz goes on to explain, "The bus boycott was the beginning of the modern civil rights movement. Once the boycott started here, it spread to other cities. It encouraged people to get involved in other ways in dealing with other aspects of segregation and discrimination."[123]

The Montgomery bus boycott signaled the beginning of a mass movement of nonviolent resistance that continued through the 1960s. As states and localities simply ignored federal laws requiring desegregation, nonviolent resistance—as preached by Martin Luther King Jr.—became the weapon by which blacks would win their rights, one establishment, one neighborhood, and one city at a time.

"My father pointed out that nonviolence means more than the absence of physical violence," Dexter Scott King, one of King's sons, said. "Nonviolence is not passive, but a courageous, active resistance to injustice. It is a way of life reflected in thought and deed, a method of conducting yourself in all of your affairs."[124]

Martin Luther King Jr.'s role in the boycott catapulted him into the national spotlight. He used his newfound fame to fight for equality for his people. In February 1957, King joined with other preachers to establish the Southern Christian Leadership Conference (SCLC) and was elected its first president. The SCLC became a leader in organizing nonviolent demonstrations to make changes throughout the South.

King continued to play a preeminent role in the fight for civil rights and, in 1964, won the Nobel Peace Prize for his efforts. In 1968, King was shot and killed in Memphis, Tennessee, but his legacy of nonviolent resistance lived on among civil rights leaders.

Martin Luther King Jr., shown here at a civil rights march, won the Nobel Peace Prize in 1964 for his efforts to secure civil rights for African Americans.

Martin Luther King Jr.

◼

On April 4, 1968, Martin Luther King Jr. was shot and killed while standing on a balcony in Memphis, Tennessee. Perhaps more than any other individual, King had changed the world in which African Americans lived. Donnie Williams, a Montgomery reverend who spent many years interviewing boycott participants, and author Wayne Greenhaw sum up King's influence on the civil rights movement.

> Dr. Martin Luther King, Jr., was hailed throughout the nation as a great leader. He spoke to overflowing crowds from Miami to New York, and from Seattle to Washington, D.C. He traveled to India, Europe, and South America. He was welcomed in capitals throughout the world, became the guest of royalty, and had an audience with the pope.
>
> Less than a decade after the birth of the civil rights movement in Montgomery, King was awarded the Nobel Peace Prize. In his acceptance speech, he spoke of the long and tortuous road between Montgomery, Alabama, and Oslo, Norway. He said he considered the award "profound recognition that nonviolence is the answer to the crucial political and moral questions of our time."

Donnie Williams and Wayne Greenhaw, *The Thunder of Angels: The Montgomery Bus Boycott and the People Who Broke the Back of Jim Crow.* Chicago: Lawrence Hill, 2006, p. 268.

The Power of Nonviolent Resistance

The Montgomery bus boycott was by no means the first time that Americans had fought for their civil rights. The battle for racial equality had been going on since before the nation's founding—when the first Africans stepped onto the continent as slaves. But it earned itself a place in history as the first of its kind.

The boycott demonstrated the power of a community-based protest. Despite the mayor's continued claims that it was being led by outside agitators, the Montgomery boycott was local in nature. Its strength lay in the fact that it was a grassroots effort. Local leaders sought out the wider black community to make decisions. Hare points out the importance of presenting a united front: "This is not to say that frictions did not arise in the Montgomery movement; they did, and sometimes they were serious. . . . But for the most part, those schisms were set aside for the good of the cause or at least kept within the movement, and a united image was projected to the outside."[125]

But perhaps the most important contribution of the Montgomery bus boycott was its legacy of nonviolent resistance. The success of the boycotters proved that nonviolent resistance could be a powerful tool in blacks' fight for equality. In the years to come, African Americans tested the power of nonviolent resistance in cities throughout the South.

On February 1, 1960, four black college students sat at the all-white lunch counter at a Woolworth's in Greensboro, South Carolina. When they ordered food, the white server behind the counter refused them service and asked them to leave. The students refused to leave. The next day, other students followed their example. Twenty-four students took part in the sit-in at the Woolworth's lunch counter.

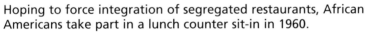

Hoping to force integration of segregated restaurants, African Americans take part in a lunch counter sit-in in 1960.

In the weeks that followed, sit-ins were staged in other southern cities. Whites sometimes joined blacks at the lunch counters and restaurant tables. Following the tactics of nonviolent resistance, the protesters sat quietly but resolutely until they were either served their food or arrested and taken to jail. By the year's end, seventy thousand

Rosa Parks: Beyond the Boycott

Rosa Parks was among the many African Americans to lose her job during the Montgomery bus boycott. Although the department store where she worked never said that they fired her because of the role she played, it laid her off when the boycott was just a few days old. Her husband, Raymond, a successful barber, lost most of his white customers because they did not want to get haircuts from a boycott participant—especially one whose wife had played such a leading role in starting all the trouble.

Following the boycott, Rosa Parks continued to fight for civil rights. In 1957, she and her husband moved to Detroit, Michigan, where she served on the staff of U.S. Representative John Conyers.

After the death of her husband in 1977, Parks founded the Rosa and Raymond Parks Institute for Self-Development. The Institute sponsors a program called Pathways to Freedom for youths between eleven and eighteen years old. Participants travel across the country tracing the Underground Railroad, visiting the scenes of critical events in the civil rights movement, and learning about America's history.

Rosa Parks continued her fight for civil rights as a speaker and role model. On several occasions, she returned to Montgomery and other parts of the South to work with Martin Luther King Jr. and other civil rights advocates. She received numerous awards for her civil rights activism, including the Presidential Medal of Freedom and the Congressional Gold Medal. The Southern Christian Leadership Council established an annual Rosa Parks Freedom Award in her honor.

When asked if she was happy living in retirement, Rosa Parks replied, "I do the very best I can to look upon life with optimism and hope and looking forward to a better day, but I don't think there is any such thing as complete happiness. It pains me that there is still a lot of Klan activity and racism. I think when you say you're happy,

people had participated in sit-in demonstrations, calling attention to the unfair segregationist practices that still existed in restaurants and other places throughout the South.

In 1961, black and white freedom riders joined together to practice nonviolent resistance to protest segregation on trains and

Rosa Parks continued to fight for civil rights for many years.

you have everything that you need and everything that you want, and nothing more to wish for. I haven't reached that stage yet."

On October 24, 2005, Rosa Parks died in Detroit. She was ninety-two. Thousands came to pay their respects at her funeral. Aretha Franklin was among those who sang a tribute to her; former president Bill Clinton was among those who spoke at the funeral. Her casket was placed in the rotunda of the United States Capitol, an honor usually reserved for U.S. presidents and other high-ranking officials. She thereby became the first woman in American history to lie in state at the Capitol.

Her work lives on through the Rosa and Raymond Parks Institute for Self-Development and in the many people who remember and seek to emulate her quiet strength.

Quoted in the Academy of Achievement, "Rosa Parks Biography." www.achievement.org/autodoc/page/par0bio-1.

buses. They openly defied the Jim Crow seating arrangements: White passengers took seats in the rear; black riders sat up front. Whenever they stopped at a bus terminal, the whites waited in the areas designated for blacks, while the blacks waited in "whites only" sections.

Success

The calm reserve of civil rights activists gradually broke down barriers to equal rights. The fight was won in the U.S. Congress, which passed landmark legislation in the mid-1960s. The fight for civil rights continued throughout the 1960s. In 1964, Lyndon B. Johnson passed the Civil Rights Act outlawing segregation and discrimination in restaurants, theaters, hotels, and other public places, as well as protecting citizens' rights to equal opportunities in employment. The next year, Congress passed the Voting Rights Act, making illegal poll taxes, literacy tests, and any other actions that states and localities had used to keep blacks from voting.

The fight was also won in the courtroom. *Brown v. Board of Education* was a landmark victory in the fight against discrimination. In courtrooms throughout America, judges and juries no longer sided with whites who violated the rights of African Americans.

Most important, the fight was won on the streets of America, by courageous people like the blacks who walked the streets of Montgomery day after day, in rain, sleet, and the hot summer heat. "When your mind is made up and your heart is fixed, then your feet are ready for traveling. God fixed our hearts,"[126] explains Donnie Williams, a Montgomery citizen who later wrote a book about the boycott.

The boycott might not have succeeded without the single act of defiance by someone like Rosa Parks. It might not have succeeded without the dedication of committed civil rights activists like E.D. Nixon and Jo Ann Robinson. It might not have succeeded without the charismatic leadership of someone like Martin Luther King Jr. It might not have succeeded without someone like Gandhi demonstrating the power of nonviolent resistance. But it assuredly would not have succeeded without the tireless sacrifice and determination of thousands of people whose names are unknown.

Rosa Parks died on October 24, 2005, at the age of ninety-two. Thousands of people flocked to her funeral to pay their last respects. Among them were some of the most famous civil rights activists and political leaders in America. Hundreds of people spoke of her quiet commitment to civil rights. President Bill Clinton was among those to give an address at her funeral. But it was Johnnie Carr, a lifelong friend of Rosa Parks, who most succinctly summed up Parks's role in history: "A woman sat down and the world turned around."[127]

Notes

Introduction: Rosa Parks Refuses to Move

1. Quoted in Henry Hampton and Steve Fayer, *Voices of Freedom: An Oral History of the Civil Rights Movement from the 1950s Through the 1980s.* New York: Bantam, 1990, p. 20.
2. Quoted in Bettye Collier-Thomas and V.P. Franklin, ed., *Sisters in the Struggle: African American Women in the Civil Rights–Black Power Movement.* New York: New York University Press, 2001, p. 61.
3. Quoted in Anne Schraff, *Rosa Parks: "Tired of Giving In."* Berkeley Heights, NJ: Enslow, 2005, p. 62.
4. Quoted in Schraff, *Rosa Parks*, p. 61.
5. Zita Allen, *Black Women Leaders of the Civil Rights Movement.* New York: Franklin Watts, 1996, p. 56.
6. Quoted in Herbert Kohl, *She Would Not Be Moved: How We Tell the Story of Rosa Parks and the Montgomery Bus Boycott.* New York: New Press, 2007, p. xiii.

Chapter One: Life in the Jim Crow South

7. Quoted in FindLaw, "U.S. Supreme Court, *Plessy v. Ferguson.*" http://caselaw.lp.findlaw.com /scripts/getcase.pl?court=US&vol= 163&invol=537.
8. Quoted in LawBuzz, "'Separate but Equal': *Plessy v. Ferguson,* 1896." www.lawbuzz.com/can_ you/plessy/plessy.htm.
9. C. Vann Woodward, *The Strange Career of Jim Crow*, 3rd ed. New York: Oxford University Press, 1974, p. 97.
10. Woodward, *The Strange Career of Jim Crow*, p. 100.
11. Woodward, *The Strange Career of Jim Crow*, p. 98.
12. Quoted in Milton Meltzer, *There Comes a Time: The Struggle for Civil Rights.* New York: Random House, 2001, p. 54.
13. Quoted in J. Morgan Kousser, "The Poll Tax," California Institute of Technology. www.hss.caltech.edu/ ~kousser/dictionary%20entries/po ll%20tax.pdf.
14. Woodward, *The Strange Career of Jim Crow*, p. 142.
15. Quoted in Donnie Williams and Wayne Greenhaw, *The Thunder of Angels: The Montgomery Bus Boycott and the People Who Broke the Back of Jim Crow.* Chicago: Lawrence Hill, 2006, p. 41.
16. Quoted in Meltzer, *There Comes a Time*, p. 48.

17. Woodward, *The Strange Career of Jim Crow*, p. 107.

18. Quoted in Clayborne Carson, David J. Garrow, Gerald Gill, Vincent Harding, and Darlene Clark Hine, eds., *The Eyes on the Prize Civil Rights Reader: Documents, Speeches, and Firsthand Accounts from the Black Freedom Struggle, 1954–1990*. New York: Penguin, 1991, pp. 25–26.

19. Quoted in Hampton and Fayer, *Voices of Freedom*, pp. 18–19.

20. Quoted in Hampton and Fayer, *Voices of Freedom*, p. 18.

21. Quoted in Hampton and Fayer, *Voices of Freedom*, p. 19.

22. Allen, *Black Women Leaders of the Civil Rights Movement*, p. 57.

23. Jo Ann Gibson Robinson, *The Montgomery Bus Boycott and the Women Who Started It: The Memoir of Jo Ann Gibson Robinson*. Knoxville: University of Tennessee Press, 1987, p. 39.

24. Robinson, *The Montgomery Bus Boycott and the Women Who Started It*, p. 36.

25. Quoted in Williams and Greenhaw, *The Thunder of Angels*, p. 14.

26. Quoted in Hampton and Fayer, *Voices of Freedom*, p. 19.

Chapter Two: Seeds of Resistance

27. Quoted in Meltzer, *There Comes a Time*, p. 51.

28. Quoted in National Association for the Advancement of Colored People, "History." www.naacp.org/about/history/howbegan/.

29. Quoted in Library of Congress Exhibitions, "Platform Adopted by the National Negro Committee." www.loc.gov/exhibits/brown/images/br0008s.jpg.

30. Williams and Greenhaw, *The Thunder of Angels*, p. 40.

31. Williams and Greenhaw, *The Thunder of Angels*, pp. 37–38.

32. Quoted in Carson et al., *The Eyes on the Prize Civil Rights Reader*, p. 31.

33. Quoted in About: African-American History, "Brown v. Board of Education." http://afroamhistory. about.com/library/bl brown_v_board.htm.

34. Quoted in U.S. Department of State, InfoUSA, "Basic Readings in U.S. Democracy: *Brown v. Board of Education* (1954)." http://usinfo.state.gov /usa/infousa/facts/democ rac/36.

35. Quoted in Carson et al., *The Eyes on the Prize Civil Rights Reader*, p. 36.

36. Quoted in Patrick L. Cooney, "Montgomery, Later Years, 1950–1952." www.vernonjohns. org/tcal001/vjmontlt.html.

37. Kai Friese, *Rosa Parks: The Movement Organizes*. Englewood Cliffs, NJ: Silver Burdett, 1990, p. 39.

38. Quoted in Carson et al., *The Eyes on the Prize Civil Rights Reader*, p. 45.

39. Quoted in Kenneth M. Hare, *They Walked to Freedom, 1955–1956: The Story of the Montgomery Bus Boycott*. Champaign, Il: Spotlight Press, 2005, p. 4.

40. Herbert Kohl, *She Would Not Be Moved: How We Tell the Story of Rosa Parks and the Montgomery Bus Boycott.* New York: New Press, 2007, p. 17.
41. Quoted in Hare, *They Walked to Freedom*, pp. 10–12.

Chapter Three: The Boycott Begins

42. Quoted in Collier-Thomas and Franklin, *Sisters in the Struggle*, p. 63.
43. Quoted in Collier-Thomas and Franklin, *Sisters in the Struggle*, p. 64.
44. Quoted in Williams and Greenhaw, *The Thunder of Angels*, p. 52.
45. Quoted in Collier-Thomas and Franklin, *Sisters in the Struggle*, p. 65.
46. Quoted in Hare, *They Walked to Freedom*, p. 21.
47. Quoted in Hampton and Fayer, *Voices of Freedom*, p. 22.
48. Quoted in Hampton and Fayer, *Voices of Freedom*, p. 22.
49. Quoted in Peter B. Levy, ed., *Documentary History of the Modern Civil Rights Movement.* Westport, CT: Greenwood, 1992, p. 57.
50. Quoted in Hampton and Fayer, *Voices of Freedom*, p. 23.
51. Quoted in Hampton and Fayer, *Voices of Freedom*, p. 21.
52. Quoted in Collier-Thomas and Franklin, *Sisters in the Struggle*, p. 66.
53. Levy, *Documentary History of the Modern Civil Rights Movement*, p. 8.
54. Quoted in Collier-Thomas and Franklin, *Sisters in the Struggle*, pp. 67–68.
55. Robinson, *The Montgomery Bus Boycott and the Women Who Started It*, p. 20.
56. Quoted in Hampton and Fayer, *Voices of Freedom*, p. 23.
57. Quoted in Collier-Thomas and Franklin, *Sisters in the Struggle*, p. 66.
58. Quoted in Friese, *Rosa Parks*, p. 64.
59. Quoted in Russell Freedman, *Freedom Walkers: The Story of the Montgomery Bus Boycott.* New York: Holiday House, 2006, p. 42.
60. Quoted in Freedman, *Freedom Walkers*, p. 42.
61. Quoted in Carson et al., *The Eyes on the Prize Civil Rights Reader*, p. 47.
62. Quoted in Collier-Thomas and Franklin, *Sisters in the Struggle*, p. 70.
63. Quoted in Carson et al., *The Eyes on the Prize Civil Rights Reader*, p. 53.
64. Quoted in Friese, *Rosa Parks*, p. 67.
65. Hare, *They Walked to Freedom*, p. 28.
66. Quoted in Collier-Thomas and Franklin, *Sisters in the Struggle*, p. 70.
67. Quoted in Carson et al., *The Eyes on the Prize Civil Rights Reader*, p. 53.
68. Martin Luther King Jr., *Stride Toward Freedom.* New York: Harper and Row, 1958, pp. 53–54.

Chapter Four: The Boycott Continues

69. Quoted in Kohl, *She Would Not Be Moved*, p. 36.
70. Robinson, *The Montgomery Bus Boycott and the Women Who Started It*, p. 43.

71. Ken Hare, "Overview," *They Changed the World, 1955–1956: The Story of the Montgomery Bus Boycott.* www.montgomeryboy cott.com/article_overview.htm.

72. Robinson, *The Montgomery Bus Boycott and the Women Who Started It*, p. 42.

73. Quoted in Collier-Thomas and Franklin, *Sisters in the Struggle*, p. 72.

74. Williams and Greenhaw, *The Thunder of Angels*, p. 116.

75. Quoted in Hare, "Overview."

76. Quoted in Joe Azbell, "End to Free Taxi Service Requested by Mayor Gayle," *Montgomery Advertiser*, January 25, 1956, p. 1A. http://nl. newsbank.com/nl-search/we/Archives ?p_action=doc&p_docid=10D160 2162CA43E8&p_docnum=31&p_ theme=gan nett&s_site=montgom eryadver tiser&p_product=MGAB.

77. Quoted in Levy, *Documentary History of the Modern Civil Rights Movement*, p. 62.

78. Quoted in Levy, *Documentary History of the Modern Civil Rights Movement*, p. 63.

79. Quoted in Hampton and Fayer, *Voices of Freedom*, p. 30.

80. Quoted in Collier-Thomas and Franklin, *Sisters in the Struggle*, p. 73.

81. Quoted in Scholastic.com, "The Life and Words of Martin Luther King, Jr." http://content.scholastic.com/ browse/article.jsp?id=4802.

82. Quoted in Williams and Greenhaw, *The Thunder of Angels*, p. 127.

83. Quoted in Williams and Greenhaw, *The Thunder of Angels*, p. 123.

84. Quoted in Levy, *A Documentary History of the Modern Civil Rights Movement*, p. 59.

85. Quoted in Hampton and Fayer, *Voices of Freedom*, p. 28.

86. Quoted in Meltzer, *There Comes a Time*, pp. 95–96.

87. Quoted in Williams and Greenhaw, *The Thunder of Angels*, p. 134.

88. Quoted in Williams and Greenhaw, *The Thunder of Angels*, p. 135.

89. Quoted in Hampton and Fayer, *Voices of Freedom*, p. 31.

90. Quoted in Williams and Greenhaw, *The Thunder of Angels*, p. 87.

91. Quoted in Jannell McGrew, "Sarah Herbert," *They Changed the World, 1955–56: The Story of the Montgomery Bus Boycott.* www. montgomeryboycott.com/profile _herbert.htm.

92. Quoted in Williams and Greenhaw, *The Thunder of Angels*, p. 86.

93. Quoted in Williams and Greenhaw, *The Thunder of Angels*, p. 87.

94. Quoted in Williams and Greenhaw, *The Thunder of Angels*, p. 146.

95. Quoted in Hare, "Overview."

96. Quoted in Hare, "Overview."

97. Quoted in Hare, "Overview."

98. Quoted in Associated Press, "Negroes Form New Group Replacing NAACP," *Montgomery Advertiser*, June 6, 1956. www. montgomery boycott.com/article_560606_new group.htm.

99. Quoted in Williams and Green-haw, *The Thunder of Angels*, p. 224.
100. Quoted in Associated Press, "Negroes Form New Group Replacing NAACP."

Chapter Five: Victory

101. Quoted in Williams and Green-haw, *The Thunder of Angels*, p. 237.
102. Quoted in Williams and Greenhaw, *The Thunder of Angels*, p. 237.
103. Quoted in Williams and Greenhaw, *The Thunder of Angels*, p. 239.
104. Quoted in Bob Ingram, "Supreme Court Outlaws Bus Segregation," *Montgomery Advertiser*, November 14, 1955. www.montgomeryboycott.com.
105. Freedman, *Freedom Walkers*, p. 84.
106. Quoted in Williams and Greenhaw, *The Thunder of Angels*, p. 243.
107. Quoted in Hampton and Fayer, *Voices of Freedom*, pp. 25–26.
108. Quoted in Freedman, *Freedom Walkers*, p. 80.
109. Quoted in Bob Ingram, "Supreme Court Outlaws Bus Segregation," *Montgomery Adviser*, November 14, 1955. www.montgomeryboycott.com.
110. Quoted in Williams and Green-haw, *The Thunder of Angels*, p. 245.
111. Quoted in Associated Press, "Lawmakers Study Means of Ducking Court's Bus Desegregation Ruling," *Montgomery Advertiser*, November 18, 1956. www.montgomeryboycott.com/

article_561118_ducking.htm.
112. Quoted in Associated Press, "Lawmakers Study Means of Ducking Court's Bus Desegregation Ruling."
113. Quoted in Carson et al., *The Eyes on the Prize Civil Rights Reader*, p. 57.
114. Quoted in Williams and Green-haw, *The Thunder of Angels*, p. 250.
115. Quoted in Carson et al., *The Eyes on the Prize Civil Rights Reader*, p. 59.
116. Quoted in Carson et al., *The Eyes on the Prize Civil Rights Reader*, p. 60.
117. Quoted in Hampton and Fayer, *Voices of Freedom*, p. 32.
118. Quoted in Hampton and Fayer, *Voices of Freedom*, p. 32.
119. Quoted in Williams and Green-haw, *The Thunder of Angels*, p. 255.
120. Quoted in Williams and Green-haw, *The Thunder of Angels*, p. 251.
121. Quoted in Williams and Green-haw, *The Thunder of Angels*, p. 262.
122. Williams and Greenhaw, *The Thunder of Angels*, p. 269.
123. Quoted in Jannell McGrew, "Rev. Robert Graetz," *They Changed the World, 1955–1956: The Story of the Montgomery Bus Boycott.* www.montgomeryboycott.com/ profile_graetz.htm.
124. Quoted in Jannell McGrew, "The

Reverend Martin Luther King, Jr.," *They Changed the World, 1955–1956: The Story of the Montgomery Bus Boycott.* www.montgomeryboycott.com/bio_ml king.htm.

125. Hare, *They Walked to Freedom*, pp. 125–26.

126. Quoted in Deborah Willoughby, "Rev. Donnie Williams," *They Changed the World, 1955–1956:* *The Story of the Montgomery Bus Boycott.* www.montgomery boy cott.com/profile_dwilliams. htm.

127. Quoted in Jannell McGrew, "Close Friend, Activist Has Special Perspective," Montgomery Advertiser.com, March 30, 2007. www.montgomeryadvertiser.com /apps/pbcs.dll/article?AID=/9999 9999/NEWS/61113023/1001.

Chronology

February 4, 1913
Rosa Parks is born Rosa Louise Mc-Cauley in Tuskegee, Alabama, to James McCauley, a carpenter, and Leona McCauley, a teacher.

December 1, 1955
Rosa Parks, a forty-two-year-old seamstress and an NAACP member, is arrested and charged with violating bus segregation laws.

December 2, 1955
Local African American leaders agree to boycott the buses and distribute a flyer asking African Americans to stay off the buses the following Monday, December 5.

December 5, 1955
African Americans, led by the newly created Montgomery Improvement Association (MIA), stage a boycott of city buses. Several thousand African Americans attend a mass meeting at Holt Street Baptist Church and vote to continue the boycott.

Rosa Parks is convicted of violating bus segregation laws and fined ten dollars, plus a court fee of four dollars.

December 13, 1955
The MIA begins its carpool system.

January 9, 1956
Negotiations between the MIA and city leaders reach a stalemate.

January 23, 1956
The city announces a "get tough" policy.

January 26, 1956
Martin Luther King Jr. is arrested for speeding.

January 30, 1956
The Kings' home is bombed. King calms the angry crowd that gathers outside his home by preaching the importance of nonviolence.

February 1, 1956
Fred Gray and Charles Langford file a lawsuit (*Browder v. Gayle*) on behalf of four female plaintiffs who had been treated unfairly on Montgomery's buses because of their race.

February 21, 1956
More than eighty leaders and partici-pants of the Montgomery bus boycott, including Rosa Parks and Martin Luther King Jr., are arrested for con-spiring to stage a boycott.

March 19, 1956
King is found guilty of breaking boy-cott laws and is sentenced to pay a five-hundred-dollar fine or spend over a year in jail.

June 4, 1956

In *Browder v. Gayle*, federal judges rule that the city and state bus segregation laws are unconstitutional.

November 13, 1956

The U.S. Supreme Court upholds the lower court's ruling, declaring Montgomery's bus segregation laws to be illegal.

November 14, 1956

The court declares that MIA's carpool system is illegal.

December 20, 1956

The Supreme Court's ruling takes effect, and Montgomery's African American community ends the boycott.

December 21, 1956

Led by Martin Luther King Jr. and other leaders of the boycott, black citizens return to Montgomery's buses, which are integrated for the first time.

October 24, 2005

Rosa Parks dies at the age of ninety-two. Thousands of mourners, including some of the country's most influential civil rights leaders, attend her funeral, which lasts more than seven hours.

For More Information

Books

Bettye Collier-Thomas and V.P. Franklin, eds., *Sisters in the Struggle: African American Women in the Civil Rights–Black Power Movement*. New York: New York University Press, 2001. This book about the role that black women played in the civil rights movement includes an account of the boycott written by Rosa Parks.

Kenneth C. Davis, *Don't Know Much About Rosa Parks*. New York: HarperCollins, 2005. This book of the Don't Know Much About series tells of living conditions in the Jim Crow South, Rosa Parks, and her contribution to the civil rights movement in question-and-answer format.

Russell Freedman, *Freedom Walkers: The Story of the Montgomery Bus Boycott*. New York: Holiday House, 2006. This account of the Montgomery bus boycott, beautifully laid out with black-and-white photos, focuses on the leaders of the movement and the reasons behind the boycott.

Ellen Levine, *Freedom's Children: Young Civil Rights Activists Tell Their Own Stories*. New York: Putnam Juvenile, 2000. This book tells the stories of thirty children and teenagers who contributed to the civil rights movement, including Claudette Colvin, the fifteen-year-old who was arrested for violating bus segregation laws in Montgomery just months prior to Rosa Parks.

Diane McWhorter, *A Dream of Freedom: The Civil Rights Movement from 1954 to 1968*. New York: Scholastic, 2004. This Pulitzer Prize–winning author provides an account of the civil rights movement from *Brown v. Board of Education* to the assassination of Martin Luther King Jr. The chapters follow chronologically, highlighting pivotal events, people, successes, and failures of the movement; ample photographs amplify the vivid account as events unfold.

Milton Meltzer, *There Comes a Time: The Struggle for Civil Rights*. New York: Random House, 2001. This survey of the civil rights movement gives a vivid account of the Montgomery bus boycott as it spans the movement from the Middle Passage to modern days. The dramatic accounts of real people who were involved in the struggle make it an interesting read that is accessible to young people.

Rosa Parks and Jim Haskins, *Rosa Parks: My Story*. New York: Puffin, 1999. In this autobiographical account, Rosa Parks describes her childhood, her family, the many people who supported her, and the people at the forefront of the Montgomery bus boycott. Parks also corrects some of the misperceptions of what happened on that historic day when she refused to give up her seat and the events that followed.

Rosa Parks and Gregory J. Reed, *Quiet Strength*. Grand Rapids, MI: Zondervan Publishing House, 2000. This book focuses on the principles behind Rosa Parks's lifelong commitment to justice for African Americans and to equality for all. Each chapter reflects on a specific element, such as determination, faith, and pain, that served as inspiration for Parks.

Anne Schraff, *Rosa Parks: "Tired of Giving In."* Berkeley Heights, NJ: Enslow, 2005. This beautifully written biography of Rosa Parks discusses aspects of her childhood and adult experiences that contributed to her steadfast character and her act of defiance.

Web Sites
The Martin Luther King, Jr., Research and Education Institute (www.stanford.edu/group/King). Includes a plethora of papers, speeches, and books by Martin Luther King Jr., including many of King's presentations and speeches during and about the Montgomery bus boycott.

Montgomery Bus Boycott, Spartacus Educational (www.spartacus.school net.co.uk/USAmontgomeryB.htm). Offers a description and first-person accounts of the boycott that began after the arrest of Rosa Parks and caught the attention of the entire nation.

Rosa Parks Biography, Academy of Achievement: A Museum of Living History (www.achievement. org/autodoc/page/par0bio-1). This Web site includes a profile and short biography of the "mother of the civil rights movement," as well as a 1995 interview with Rosa Parks and photos taken throughout her life.

Rosa Parks: How I Fought for Civil Rights, Scholastic (http://teacher. scholastic.com/rosa/index.htm). This detailed account of Rosa Parks and the Montgomery bus boycott, aimed at seventh- and eighth-grade students, provides quotations and interview clips with Parks.

Rosa and Raymond Parks Institute for Self-Development (www.rosa parks.org/). Hosted by the institute that Rosa Parks cofounded in 1987 to encourage and inspire youth, this Web site includes a biography of Rosa Parks and a time line of the events leading up to and beyond the Montgomery bus boycott.

They Changed the World: The Story of the Montgomery Bus Boycott, MontgomeryAdvertiser.com (www.montgomeryboycott.com). This comprehensive Web site includes a time line of the events of the boycott, video clips, remembrances from people involved in the boycott, and a series of articles about the boycott published in the local newspaper in 1955 to 1956.

Index

A

Abernathy, Ralph D., 47, 78
  bombing of house of, 79
  on Jim Crow laws, 21
  on job choices for blacks, 22
Alabama
  segregation on buses law, 22
Alabama Christian Movement for Human
  Rights, 70
Allen, Zita, 8
  on racist bus drivers, 23
Arrests of boycotters, 62
Azbell, Joe, 53
  on support of boycott, 54
  support of King, 65

B

Baton Rouge, Louisiana
  bus boycott in, 35–36
Black churches
  bombing of, 79
  collection of donations for boycotters,
    59
  involvement in bus boycott, 48, 51–54
Black community, 9
*Black Women Leaders of the Civil Rights
  Movement*, 8
Blacks
  denied right to vote, 16–17
  fear of losing jobs, 18
  soldiers fight for civil rights, 32
Brooks, Thomas Edward, 24
Brotherhood of Sleeping Car Porters, 31
Browder v. Gayle, 68–69
Brown, Henry Billings, 12
Brown, Oliver, 32
Brown v. Board of Education, 30
  application to bus segregation, 68–69
  ending of school segregation, 32–34

Buchanan v. Worley, 30
Bus boycott, 8–9
  black participation in, 58–59
  bus company gives in, 62
  childrens' participation in, 74
  demands presented by, 57–58
  end of, 77–78
  lessons learned, 82–83
  NAACP's involvement in, 30
  nonviolence as a tactic of, 53–54, 83
  reaction to end of, 79–80
  start of, 44–47, 54–55
  success of, 25, 50–51, 59–60
Bus drivers
  treatment of blacks, 22–24, 37
  violence of, 24, 26
Bus service
  curtailed during boycott, 58

C

Carpools
  declared illegal, 73
  insurance companies involvement in, 70
  organizing, 58–59
  police harassment of, 61–62
  threats against, 71
Carr, Johnnie, 87
Citizens' Committee, 12
Civil Rights Act, 86
Civil War
  attitudes toward blacks and, 10
  poll tax developed during, 17
Clinton, Bill, 87
Code of Alabama, 71
Colvin, Claudette, 37
  case taken up by NAACP, 37–38, 40, 44

D

Draught, Woodson, 67

DuBois, W.E.B., 28
  poem by, 33
Durr, Clifford, 38, 42
Durr, Virginia, 60, 61

E
Edelman, Marian Wright, 8
Education
  colleges and universities open to blacks, 32
  National Negro Conference and, 29
  under Jim Crow laws, 22
Eyes on the Prize Civil Rights Reader, 20–21

F
Ferguson, John, 12
Fifteenth Amendment, 17
  National Negro Conference and, 29
Fourteenth Amendment, 69
Franklin, Pink
  case defended by NAACP, 29
Freedom Riders, 85–86
Friese, Kai, 35

G
Gandhi, Mohandas, 53, 57
Gayle, W.A. "Tacky," 60, 74
Gilmore, Georgia, 77
Graetz, Robert
  bombing of home of, 79
  on meaning of bus boycott, 80
  support of boycott, 67–68
Grandfather clauses in voting, 17
  outlawing of, 30
Gray, Fred, 38, 42, 68
  friendship with Rosa Parks, 40
  involvement in Rosa Parks case, 44, 50–51
Great Depression, 16

H
Hale, Grace, 18
Harding, Vincent
  on Jim Crow laws, 20–21
Hare, Kenneth M., 53, 58
Harlan, John
  dissenting view in *Plessy v Ferguson*, 12–14
Herbert, Sarah, 67
Highlander Folk School, 40–41

Hubbard, H.H., 47

I
Insurance companies, 70

J
Jackson, Mahalia
  experience with Jim Crow laws, 20
Jim Crow laws, 10–11
  black protests against, 35
  bus boycott ends, 62
  Connecticut bans in 1945, 32
  expansion of, 14
  in the north, 15–16
  pervasiveness of, 20–21
  use of violence to enforce, 18
Johns, Vernon
  refusal to abide by segregation, 34–35
Johnson, Lyndon B., 86
Johnson, Marshall and Edwina
  arrests of, 27–28
Johnson, Mattie, 24
  on killing of black bus rider, 25

K
King, Martin Luther, 8, 47, 78, 79
  assassination of, 82
  attempted bombing of home, 79
  on carpools, 71, 72–73
  on death threats, 68
  effect of boycott on fame, 81
  elected chair of MIA, 51–52
  eloquence of, 53
  on first boycott meeting, 54
  speech on nonviolence, 49
  on Supreme Court ruling, 72
  threats against, 64–65
  trial of, 62–63
Kohl, Herert, 41
Ku Klux Klan, 18
  during bus boycott, 64

L
Langford, Charles, 68
Law enforcement
  arrests of boycotters, 62
  beatings of disobedient blacks, 24, 27

harassment of boycotters, 61–62
  as racist, 18–19
"Letter from Birmingham Jail," 63
Levy, Peter B., 48
Literacy tests, 17
  found unconstitutional, 32
Lynching, 18

M

Minstrel shows, 11
Montgomery, Alabama
  blacks in the 1950s, 8
  bus segregation law, 22–24
  violence in, 80–81
Montgomery Improvement Association (MIA),
  51–52
  advocates non-violence, 74, 76
  monthly meetings held by, 59
  organizing of car pools, 58–59
  police harassment of, 61–62
  trial of, 71
Montgomery Voters' League, 31

N

NAACP, 26
  banning of, 70
  campaign against lynching, 29–30
  formation of, 29
  involvement in Brown v. Board of Education,
    32–34
  involvement in Claudette Colvin case, 37–38
  protests against Jim Crow, 35
  white support of, 66
National Negro Conference, 29
Nesbitt, Gussie, 74
Niagara Movement, 28
Nixon, E.D., 18, 32, 38
  bus boycott and, 47–48, 51, 73
  on end of boycott, 78
  founder of Montgomery Voters' League, 31
  response to Rosa Parks arrest, 42
  Rosa Parks case and, 43–44
  speaks out on fear, 52–53
  threats against, 65–66
Nonviolence
  in civil rights movement, 80–81, 83–84

in Montgomery bus boycott, 53–54, 74, 76

P

Parks, Raymond (husband of Rosa), 39, 47
  Scottsboro boys case and, 41
Parks, Rosa
  arrest of, 42
  on bus boycott, 45
  on bus laws, 22–23, 26
  childhood of, 39
  commitment to civil rights, 44, 84–85
  comparison to Claudette Colvin, 38–40
  death of, 86–87
  on racism today, 77
  story of being kicked off the bus, 6–8
Plessy, Homer, 12
Plessy v. Ferguson, 11–12
  as encouraging segregaton, 14–15
  unequal conditions under, 19–20
Poll tax, 16–17
Powell, Adam Clayton Jr., 32
Primary elections, 17

R

Race riot
  in Springfield, Illinois, 28
Racism, 10
  protests against, 35–36
Reconstruction, 10
Robinson, Jo Ann
  advocates bus boycott, 36–37, 44–47
  on avoiding violence, 56
  on black bus riders, 24
  on end of boycott, 77–78
  on harassment by police officers, 61–62
  newsletter produced by, 59
  on reaction of police to bus boycott, 50
  threats against, 66

S

Salt March of 1950, 57
Satyagraha, 57
Schools for blacks, 22
Scottsboro boys, 39, 41
Sears, Roebuck and Company, 32
Segregation, 19–21

beginnings of, 11
expansion of, 14–15
first laws against, 12
on railways, 12–13
reaction to end of, 79
as violating Fourteenth Amendment, 69
Separate but equal, 14
during the 1950s, 27
Slavery
developed attitude toward blacks, 10
Smiley, Glen, 78
Springfield, Illinois
race riot in, 28
"Suggestions for Integrating the Buses," 76

T

Trade unions
banning black membership, 22
They Walked to Freedom, 53
Thunder of Angels, 31
Trains
segregation of, 11–12, 13
Truman, Harry S.
banning segregation in armed forces 32

U

U.S. Constitution
did not protect blacks' rights, 11, 17
NAACP's enforcement of rights under, 30
National Negro Conference and, 29
Thirteenth and Fourteenth amendments, 14,
69–70
U.S. Supreme Court
Brown v. Board of Education, 32–34
outlawing of housing laws, 30
outlaws segregation on buses, 72–73

V

Voting, 16
intimidation tactics, 17–18
literacy tests and, 17
NAACP and, 30
Voting Rights Act, 86

W

Warren, Earl
opinion in Brown v. Board of Education, 33–34
White Citizens' Council (WCC), 64
threatens boycotters, 74
Whites,
intimidation tactics used by, 64
reaction to end of bus segregation, 79–80
response to boycott, 60–61
supporters of boycotters, 66–68
Williams, Donnie, 31, 60
on effect of boycott, 86
on violence, 80
Wilson, Woodrow, 16
condemnation of lynching, 30
Women's Political Council (WPC)
ending segregation on buses, 36–37
involvement in bus boycott, 46–47
Woodward, C. Vann
on expansion of segregation, 15
on Jim Crow laws, 19
on train segregation, 14
on voting intimidation, 17
Woolworth's
lunch counter protests, 83–84
World War I, 33
World War II
effect on segregation, 32

Picture Credits

Cover photo: © Bettmann/Corbis
AP Images, 19, 38, 43, 51, 52, 57
© Bettmann/Corbis, 15, 23, 40, 65
© Corbis, 21
Don Cravens/Time & Life Pictures/Getty Images, 48, 62, 67, 69, 73, 75, 78
George Dabrowski/Getty Images, 85
Herbert Gehr/Getty Images, 31
Hulton Archive/Getty Images, 35
Carl Iwasaki/Time & Life Pictures/Getty Images, 34
The Library of Congress, 11
Francis Miller/Time & Life Pictures/Getty Images, 16
© Jack Moebes/Corbis, 7
© Flip Schulke/Corbis, 81
Donald Uhrbrock/Time & Life Pictures/Getty Images, 83
Greg Villet/Time & Life Pictures/Getty Images, 61

About the Author

Lydia Bjornlund is a consultant and freelance writer, focusing primarily on issues related to American history and government. She is the author of numerous books for adults and children. She also has experience as an English teacher and has written curriculum and training materials on a wide range of topics. This is her seventh book for Lucent Books.

Ms. Bjornlund earned a master of education degree at Harvard University and a bachelor of arts degree at Williams College. She lives in Oakton, Virginia, with her husband, Gerry Hoetmer, and their twins, Jake and Sophia.